The Ultimate Estonian Cookbook

111 Dishes From Estonia To Cook Right Now

Slavka Bodic

Copyright @2024

All rights reserved. No part of this book may be reproduced in any form without writing permission in writing from the author. Reviewers may quote brief passages in reviews.

No part of this publication may be reproduced or transmitted in any form or by any means, mechanical or electronic, including photocopying or recording, or by any information storage and retrieval system, or transmitted by email without permission in writing from the publisher. While all attempts have been made to verify the information provided in this publication, neither the author nor the publisher assumes any responsibility for errors, omissions or contrary interpretations of the subject matter herein.

This book is for entertainment purposes only. The views expressed are those of the author alone and should not be taken as expert instruction or command. The reader is responsible for his or her actions. Adherence to all applicable laws and regulations, including international, federal, state and local governing professional licensing, business practices, advertising, and all other aspects of doing business in US, Canada or any other jurisdiction is the sole responsibility of the purchaser or reader.

Neither the author nor the publisher assumes any responsibility or liability whatsoever on the behalf of the purchaser or reader of these materials. Any perceived slight of any individual or organization is purely unintentional. Similarity with already published recipes is possible.

Imprint: Independently published

Please sign up for free Balkan and Mediterranean recipes:
www.balkanfood.org

Introduction

Are you a foodie who loves to enjoy different cuisines with exotic flavors? Do you love to explore new cultures and culinary practices? Have you ever wondered about Estonian food or tried it before? Do you want to recreate those authentic Estonian flavors at home?

Then this **Ultimate 111 Estonian Cookbook** is just the perfect read for you. Estonian food, like its history and diverse culture, is far more interesting than you think. The cuisine offers lots of delicious desserts, salads, soups, appetizers, etc. All Estonian recipes are prepared using a mix of rich and delicious ingredients using unique cooking techniques. What is most interesting about Estonian cuisine is that it's considered highly nutritious, and by reading this cookbook, you'll know why!

Estonian cuisine is a unique blend of traditional and modern flavors influenced by the country's geography, history, and cultural heritage. Rooted in its agricultural heritage, Estonian cuisine features simple, wholesome ingredients such as potatoes, grains, fish, and dairy products. Classic Estonian dishes include kama, a traditional porridge made from roasted barley, rye, and pea flour; herring served in various ways, such as pickled, smoked, or marinated; and kohuke, a sweet curd snack. Pork is also a popular meat in Estonian cuisine, often used in dishes like verivorst, blood sausage, and sült, a jellied meat dish. Additionally, Estonian cuisine features an abundance of foraged ingredients, such as mushrooms and berries, which are used in a variety of dishes and preserves. Overall,

Estonian cuisine is characterized by its simplicity, focus on local ingredients, and traditional flavors that reflect the country's rich culinary heritage.

In this Estonian cuisine cookbook, you can find a complete range of Estonian sides and Entrée meals compiled and organized in this one cookbook. The goal was to bring you the most famous Estonian recipes in the simplest way possible. All the recipes are therefore written with easy-to-follow instructions and simple-to-buy ingredients. From the classic Estonian Kasha to Sirniki and Ukha, you can discover all the traditional and most popular meals from Eastern Europe.

Living for a year in Estonia and traveling to its different parts, I was greatly fascinated by the diversity of flavors and cooking methods used in those areas. Experiencing Estonian cuisine and learning to cook various Estonian meals was one thing that I wanted to share with all my avid cookbook readers. And this cookbook comes after my seven years of learning about the diverse Estonian culinary culture. All the 111 recipes shared in this cookbook are enough to create an entire Estonian menu of your own. With the help of these recipes, you can enjoy special flavors on special occasions, or you can just surprise your loved ones with authentic Estonian flavors.

Here's a summary of what you can find in this cookbook:

- Something about Estonia and Estonian cuisine
- Estonian Breakfast Recipes
- Snacks
- Sides and Salad Recipes
- Soup and Stew Recipes
- Main Dishes and Entrees
- Estonian Desserts and Drinks

Let's try all these Estonian Recipes and recreate a complete menu to celebrate the amazing Estonian flavors and aromas.

TABLE OF CONTENTS

INTRODUCTION 3
WHY ESTONIAN CUISINE? 10
ESTONIA 12
BREAKFAST 15
    WHOLE WHEAT BREAD (SEPIK) 16
    ESTONIAN WAFFLES 18
    PANCAKES (PANNKOOK) 20
    KRINGEL 22
    ESTONIAN BREAD (NISULEIB) 25
    ESTONIAN CARROT BREAD (PORGANDILEIB) 27
    POPPY SEED BREAD (MOONILEIB) 29
    ESTONIAN SEED BREAD (SEEMNELEIB) 31
    ESTONIAN PUMPKIN BREAD (KÕRVITSALEIB) 33
    ESTONIAN OAT BREAD (KAERALEIB) 35
    MARTSIPAN (MARZIPAN) 37
    ESTONIAN SWEET BUN (SAIAKE) 39
    TRADITIONAL ESTONIAN BREAD (KAMA LEIB) 41
    BLUEBERRY PORRIDGE (MUSTIKAPUDER) 43
    BLACK RYE BREAD (RUKKILEIB) 45
    ESTONIAN PORRIDGE 47
    MASHED EGGS (MUNAVÕI) 49
    ESTONIAN SAUSAGE (EESTI VORST) 50
    ESTONIAN OMELET 52
    POTATO PANCAKES 54
    ESTONIAN MODERN PORRIDGE (HOMMIKUPUDER) 55
    ESTONIAN VEGETABLE OMELET (JUURVILJAOMLETT) 57
    ESTONIAN BARLEY PORRIDGE (ODERPUDER) 59
SNACKS 61
    BROAD BEANS FRITTERS (HÕRGUD KÕRTPOOLAKESED) 62
    ESTONIAN CURD SNACK (KOHUPIIMAKREEM) 64
    ESTONIAN SEMLA (VASTLAKUKKEL) 66
    ESTONIAN SPRAT SANDWICH (SPROTIVÕILEIB) 69
    POTATO CHIPS (KARTULIKRÕPSUD) 71

 Onion Rings (Sibulakrõpsud) 73
 Roasted Grain Snack (Kama) 75
 Wild Garlic Chips (Karulauguviilud) 77
 Canned Moose Meat (Põdralihakonserv) 79
 Estonian herring slices (Kiluviilud) 81
 Estonian breadsticks (Leivasnäkid) 83
 Estonian pickles (Hapukurk) 85
 Kohuke 87
 Kama Kottidega 89
 Ham and Cheese Buns 90
 Estonian Potato Balls (Kartulipallid) 92
 Estonian carrot slices (Porgandiviilud Hapukoorega) 94
 Marinated Mushrooms 95

SALADS 97

 Estonian Potato Salad 98
 Beet Salad (Punasepeedisalat) 100
 Mushroom Salad (Seenesalat) 102
 Cucumber Salad (Kurgisalat) 104
 Herring Salad (Suitsusilli Salat) 106
 Carrot Salad (Porgandisalat) 108
 Cabbage Salad (Kapsasalat) 110
 Tomato And Cucumber Salad (Tomati-Kurgisalat) 112
 Mixed Salad (Segasalat) 114

SOUPS 116

 Pea Soup (Hernesupp) 117
 Estonian Pumpkin Puree Soup (Kõrvitsapüreesupp) 119
 Mushroom Soup (Seenesupp) 121
 Estonian Pea Soup (Kaalika-Hernesupp) 123
 Fish Soup (Kalasupp) 125
 Beet Soup (Borsisupp) 127
 Sauerkraut Soup (Hapukapsasupp) 129
 Barley Soup (Odrasupp) 131
 Cabbage Soup 133
 Estonian sauerkraut soup (Hapukapsasupp) 135

MAIN DISHES 137

 Pork and Sauerkraut Stew (Seakapsahautis) 138
 Beef Stew (Hakklihahautis) 140
 Chicken and Vegetable Stew (Kana- Ja Köögiviljahautis) 142

- Mushroom and Potato Stew (Seene- ja Kartulihautis) 144
- Lamb Stew (Lamba- või Tallehautis) 146
- Estonian Fish Stew (Kalaroog) 148
- Bean Stew (Oa- või Hernesupp) 150
- Estonian Mushroom Rice Casserole (Seeneriis) 152
- Estonian Cabbage and Rice Casserole (Kapsa-Riisivorm) 154
- Estonian Rice and Vegetable Stir-Fry (Riis ja Köögiviljad Wokis) 156
- Estonian Oven-Baked Potatoes (Ahjukartulid) 158
- Veggie Mince Sauce 160
- Kõrvitsakotletid 162
- Kama-Kotletid 164
- Kapsarullid 166
- Kaalikapirukas 168
- Juurviljapada 171
- Röstitud Juurviljad 173
- Mushroom Stew (Seenehautis) 175
- Rice and Chicken Casserole (Kana-Riisivorm) 177
- Pajaroog 179
- Estonian Beef Meatballs (Lihapallid) 181
- Estonian Beef Roulades (Räimerullid) 183
- Estonian Beef Patties (Hakklihakotletid) 185
- Estonian Rolled Herring (Räimerullid) 187
- Beef and Potato Casserole 189
- Marmorliha 191
- Chicken Pate 193
- Chicken and Pasta Casserole 195
- Estonian Chicken Wraps (Kanawrapid) 197
- Grilled Pork Chops (Grillitud Seakarbonaad) 199
- Beef and Vegetable Skewers (Veiseliha- ja Köögiviljavardad) 201
- Veggie and Halloumi Skewers 203

DESSERT **204**

- Sweet Braided Bread 205
- Estonian Curd Cake (Kohupiimakook) 207
- Rye Bread Cake (Karask) 209
- Teddy Bear Cake (Mõmmik) 211
- Quark Cheese Cake (Kubujuustukook) 214
- Grandma's Cake (Vanaema Kook) 216
- Estonian Sheet Cake (Plaadikook) 218
- Raisin Kissel (Rosinakissell) 220
- Estonian Dessert Soup (Leivasupp) 222

Vahukoor-Kohupiimakook	224
Potato Cake (Kartulikook)	226
Kamavaht	228
Kama and Apple Cake (Kama-Õunakook)	230

DRINKS 232

Fruit Wine (Leibkonna Jook)	233
Kvas	235
Kefir	237
Estonian Morss	238
Estonian Kali Drink	239

ONE LAST THING 249

Why Estonian Cuisine?

Estonian cuisine is a unique blend of traditional and modern flavors influenced by the country's geography, history, and cultural heritage. Rooted in its agricultural heritage, Estonian cuisine features simple, wholesome ingredients such as potatoes, grains, fish, and dairy products. Classic Estonian dishes include kama, a traditional porridge made from roasted barley, rye, and pea flour; herring served in various ways, such as pickled, smoked, or marinated; and kohuke, a sweet curd snack. Pork is also a popular meat in Estonian cuisine, often used in dishes like verivorst, blood sausage, and sült, a jellied meat dish. Additionally, Estonian cuisine features an abundance of foraged ingredients, such as mushrooms and berries, which are used in a variety of dishes and preserves. Overall, Estonian cuisine is characterized by its simplicity, focus on local ingredients, and traditional flavors that reflect the country's rich culinary heritage. Estonian cuisine is a reflection of the country's agricultural heritage, with an emphasis on simple, wholesome ingredients and traditional flavors. From hearty porridges to savory sausages and tangy herring dishes to sweet treats, Estonian cuisine offers a unique and diverse culinary experience.

Kama is a traditional Estonian porridge made from roasted barley, rye, and pea flour. It is typically mixed with sour cream or buttermilk and sometimes sweetened with sugar or honey. Kama is often enjoyed as a hearty breakfast or a nutritious snack, and its unique combination of flavors and textures makes it a popular dish among Estonians.

Verivorst, also known as blood sausage, is a beloved Estonian dish that's often enjoyed during the Christmas season. It's made from a mixture of pork blood, barley or buckwheat groats, and various spices, such as black pepper, allspice, and cloves. The mixture is then stuffed into casings and boiled or fried until crispy. Verivorst is typically served with sauerkraut, lingonberry sauce, and potatoes, and its rich, savory flavors are a favorite among Estonians during the holiday festivities.

Herring is a staple ingredient in Estonian cuisine and is often served in various ways. Pickled herring, known as marineeritud heeringas, is a popular dish that features herring fillets marinated in a mixture of vinegar, sugar, and spices, such as bay leaves and cloves. Smoked herring, or suitsusilg, is another common preparation, where herring fillets are traditionally smoked over open flames, giving them a distinct smoky flavor. Marinated herring, or marineeritud sprotid, is another popular dish that features small, marinated herring fillets served with onions and sour cream. Herring is often enjoyed as an appetizer or a main course, and its tangy, briny flavors are beloved by Estonians.

Kohuke is a popular sweet treat in Estonia, often enjoyed as a snack or a dessert. It's made from curd cheese mixed with sugar and flavored with various fruits, such as berries or tropical fruits. The mixture is then covered in a thin layer of chocolate or sugar glaze, giving it a sweet and creamy texture. Kohuke comes in a variety of flavors and is often packaged in individual wrappers, making it a convenient and tasty on-the-go snack.

Estonia

Estonia, located in Northern Europe along the eastern coast of the Baltic Sea, is a small but vibrant country with a rich history and culture. Its landscape is characterized by pristine forests, serene lakes, and charming coastal areas. The people of Estonia, known as Estonians, are known for their warm hospitality, resilience, and strong connection to their natural surroundings. Estonian culture is deeply rooted in its history and folklore, with a strong emphasis on music, literature, and traditional crafts. The country is also home to many famous landmarks and destinations that attract visitors from all around the world.

One of Estonia's notable features is its stunning landscape. Forests cover nearly half of the country, making it one of the most forested countries in Europe. These lush woodlands are home to an array of wildlife, including bears, wolves, and lynxes. Estonia is also known for its vast network of lakes, with over 1,500 lakes scattered throughout the country. Lake Peipus, the fifth largest lake in Europe, is a popular destination for fishing and boating. The country's coastline, stretching over 3,700 kilometers, is dotted with picturesque coastal towns, sandy beaches, and limestone cliffs, offering breathtaking views of the Baltic Sea.

The people of Estonia, known as Estonians, are known for their friendly and welcoming nature. They have a strong connection to their land and a deep appreciation for their natural environment. Estonians have a resilient spirit, having overcome centuries of foreign rule and conflicts.

They have a strong sense of national identity and pride in their language, which is one of the few remaining Finno-Ugric languages spoken in Europe. Estonians are also known for their love of music, with choral singing being an important part of their cultural heritage. The Song Festival, held every five years in Tallinn, is a renowned event that showcases Estonian music and brings together thousands of singers from across the country.

Estonian culture is rich and diverse, shaped by its history and traditions. Folklore plays a significant role in Estonian culture, with tales of mythical creatures, legends, and superstitions passed down through generations. Traditional crafts, such as pottery, weaving, and woodwork, are highly valued and preserved in Estonia. The country's cuisine is influenced by its agricultural heritage, with a focus on simple, wholesome ingredients like potatoes, grains, fish, and dairy products. Estonian cuisine also incorporates foraged ingredients like mushrooms and berries, which are used in a variety of dishes and preserves.

Estonia is also known for its famous landmarks and destinations. The capital city of Tallinn is a UNESCO World Heritage Site, known for its well-preserved medieval architecture, cobbled streets, and historic city walls. Tallinn's Old Town, with its Gothic spires, medieval buildings, and charming squares, is a popular tourist destination that offers a glimpse into Estonia's rich history. The Lahemaa National Park, located on the northern coast, is a stunning nature reserve with ancient forests, picturesque coastal landscapes, and historic manor houses. The university town of Tartu is another famous destination, famous for its rich cultural heritage, vibrant arts scene, and historical buildings, including the iconic Tartu University building.

Breakfast

Whole Wheat Bread (Sepik)

Preparation time: 15 minutes
Cook time: 35 minutes
Nutrition facts (per serving): 142 Cal (4.9g fat, 5.2g protein, 3g fiber)

Sepik, a traditional Papua New Guinean bread made with whole wheat flour, is known for its rustic, hearty texture and rich, nutty flavor.

Ingredients (8 servings)
3 cups whole wheat flour
1 ½ cups warm water
¼ cup honey or maple syrup
2 ¼ teaspoon active dry yeast
2 teaspoons salt
2 tablespoons vegetable oil

Preparation
In a suitable mixing bowl, mix the warm water, honey (or maple syrup), and yeast. Stir until the yeast is dissolved. Let it sit for about 5 minutes until the yeast becomes frothy. Stir in the whole wheat flour, salt, and vegetable oil in the bowl with the yeast mixture. Mix well to form a dough. On a floured surface, knead this dough for about 5-7 minutes until it becomes smooth and elastic. If this dough is too sticky, you can add a little more flour, but be careful not to add too much as it may result in dense bread. Shape this dough into a ball and place it in a greased bowl.

Cover with a clean towel or plastic wrap and let it rise in a warm, draft-free place for about 1 hour until it doubles in size.

At 375°F, preheat your oven. Grease a loaf pan. Punch down the risen dough and turn it out onto a floured surface. Shape it into a loaf and place it into the greased loaf pan. Cover the loaf pan with a clean towel or plastic wrap and let this dough rise for another 30-45 minutes until it reaches the top of the pan. Once this dough has risen, place the loaf pan in the preheated oven and bake for 30-35 minutes, until the top is golden brown and the bread sounds hollow when tapped on the bottom. Remove the bread from the oven and leave it to cool in the pan for about 5 minutes, then place it onto the wire rack to cool completely before slicing and serving. Enjoy your homemade Sepik whole-wheat bread! It's perfect for sandwiches, toast, or as a side with soups and stews.

Estonian Waffles

Preparation time: 10 minutes
Cook time: 10 minutes
Nutrition facts (per serving): 258 Cal (9g fat, 1g protein, 4g fiber)

Estonian Waffles, also known as "Vahvlid" in Estonian cuisine, are delightful crispy and light waffles that are typically enjoyed as a breakfast or dessert. They're often served with whipped cream and jam, making them a perfect indulgence for special occasions or afternoon tea.

Ingredients (8 servings)
2 large eggs
½ cup granulated sugar
½ cup unsalted butter, melted
1 ½ cups all-purpose flour
1 ½ teaspoon baking powder
1 teaspoon vanilla extract
¼ teaspoon salt
1 cup whole milk
Whipped cream and jam, for serving

Preparation
In a suitable mixing bowl, whisk the eggs and sugar until well combined. Stir in the melted butter, flour, baking powder, vanilla extract, and salt in the bowl. Mix until the prepared batter is smooth and no lumps remain. Gradually stir in the milk to the prepared batter, mixing well after each addition until the prepared batter has a thick but pourable consistency. Preheat a waffle iron according to the manufacturer's instructions.

Spoon about ¼ to ½ cup of batter (depending on the size of your waffle iron) onto the hot waffle iron and spread it out evenly.

Close the waffle iron and cook the waffle until golden brown and crispy, following the instructions of your waffle iron. Carefully remove the waffle from the iron and place it on a wire rack to cool slightly. Repeat the process with the remaining batter until all the waffles are cooked. Serve the Estonian Waffles warm with whipped cream and jam on top or any other desired toppings such as fresh berries or powdered sugar. Enjoy the delicious Estonian Waffles as a sweet treat or dessert!

Pancakes (Pannkook)

Preparation time: 20 minutes
Cook time: 15 minutes
Nutrition facts (per serving): 167 Cal (5.3 fat, 11.4 protein, 0.8g fiber)

Pannkook, a popular Estonian dish, features fluffy pancakes with a slightly sour taste, typically served with sweet or savory toppings, making them a versatile and beloved treat for any time of the day.

Ingredients (8 servings)
2 cups all-purpose flour
2 cups milk
2 large eggs
¼ cup granulated sugar
½ teaspoon salt
1 teaspoon vanilla extract
¼ cup unsalted butter, melted
Additional butter or oil, for cooking
Jam, fresh berries, whipped cream, powdered sugar, for topping

Preparation
In a suitable mixing bowl, whisk the flour, milk, eggs, sugar, salt, and vanilla extract until well combined. Stir in the melted butter to the prepared batter and whisk again until the prepared batter is smooth. Heat a non-stick skillet or griddle over medium heat and lightly grease it with butter or oil. Pour about ¼ cup of batter onto the heated skillet or griddle

for each pancake. Cook until bubbles form on the surface of the pancake and the edges start to look set, about 2-3 minutes. Flip the pancake and cook for an additional 1-2 minutes on the other side, until golden brown. Remove the cooked pancake from the skillet or griddle and repeat the process with the remaining batter, adding more butter or oil as needed to prevent sticking. Serve the Pannkook pancakes hot with your favorite toppings such as jam, fresh berries, whipped cream, or powdered sugar. Enjoy your delicious Estonian pancakes!

Kringel

Preparation time: 20 minutes
Cook time: 40 minutes
Nutrition facts (per serving): 334 Cal (31g fat, 6g protein, 0.1g fiber)

Kringel is traditionally shaped into an oval ring, but you can also shape it into a circle or other desired shapes. Additionally, you can customize the filling by using different types of nuts or adding dried fruits, chocolate chips, or other sweet fillings according to your preference.

Ingredients (8 servings)
Dough
4 cups all-purpose flour
½ cup sugar, granulated
½ teaspoon salt
2 ¼ teaspoon active dry yeast
1 cup warm milk
½ cup unsalted butter, melted
2 large eggs
1 teaspoon vanilla extract

Filling
½ cup unsalted butter, softened
½ cup sugar, granulated
1 tablespoon ground cinnamon
½ cup chopped nuts (almonds, walnuts, or pecans), optional

Glaze

½ cup powdered sugar

2 tablespoons milk

1 teaspoon vanilla extract

Preparation

In a suitable mixing bowl, whisk the sugar, flour, salt, and yeast. In a separate bowl, mix the warm milk, melted butter, eggs, and vanilla extract. Mix well. Gradually Stir in the dry flour mixture, stirring until a soft dough forms. Turn this dough out onto a floured surface and knead for about 5-7 minutes until it becomes smooth and elastic. Place this dough back in the mixing bowl, cover it with a clean towel or plastic wrap, and let it rise in a warm, draft-free place for about 1 hour until it doubles in size. While this dough is rising, prepare the filling by mixing together the softened butter, sugar, cinnamon, and chopped nuts (if using) in a suitable bowl. Set aside.

At 350°F, preheat your oven. Line a baking sheet with parchment paper. Once this dough has risen, punch it down and turn it out onto a floured surface. Roll it into a rectangle about 18x12 inches. Spread the filling evenly over this dough, leaving a suitable border around the edges. Starting from one long side, tightly roll up this dough into a log, pinching the edges to seal. Carefully transfer the rolled dough onto the prepared baking sheet and shape it into a ring, pinching the ends together to seal and form a circular shape. Using sharp scissors or a knife, make cuts about ⅔ of the way through this dough at 1-inch intervals, leaving the center intact. Gently twist each section of this dough outward to create a braided effect. Bake the Kringel in the preheated oven for 25-30 minutes, until golden brown and the bread sounds hollow when tapped on the bottom.

Remove the Kringel from the oven and leave it to cool on the baking sheet for about 10 minutes, then place it onto the wire rack to cool completely. While the Kringel is cooling, prepare the glaze by whisking together the powdered sugar, milk, and vanilla extract in a suitable bowl. Once the Kringel has cooled, drizzle the glaze over the top. Slice and serve the Kringel, and enjoy this delicious Estonian sweet bread!

Estonian Bread (Nisuleib)

Preparation time: 15 minutes
Cook time: 37 minutes
Nutrition facts (per serving): 382 Cal (13g fat, 9g protein, 6g fiber)

Nisuleib, or Estonian wheat bread, is a staple in Estonian cuisine known for its hearty texture and wholesome flavor, making it a beloved accompaniment to many meals.

Ingredients (8 servings)
1 lb. wheat flour
1 teaspoon active dry yeast
1 teaspoon salt
1 teaspoon sugar
1 ¼ cup warm water
1 oz. butter, melted

Preparation
In a suitable mixing bowl, mix the wheat flour, yeast, salt, and sugar. Stir to mix well. Gradually stir in the warm water while stirring, until this dough comes together. Turn this dough out onto a floured surface and knead for about 5-7 minutes, until this dough becomes smooth and elastic. Place this dough back into the mixing bowl, cover with a clean towel, and let it rise in a warm place for about 1 hour, until it has doubled in size.

At 400°F, preheat your oven and grease a bread pan. Punch down the risen dough and turn it out onto a floured surface. Shape it into a loaf and place it into the greased bread pan. Brush the melted butter over the top of this dough. Bake the bread in the preheated oven for 25-30 minutes, until it turns golden brown on top and sounds hollow when tapped on the bottom. Remove the bread from the oven and leave it to cool in the pan for a few minutes, then place it onto the wire rack to cool completely.

Once the bread has cooled, slice it and serve as desired. Enjoy your homemade Estonian wheat bread! It's perfect for sandwiches, toast, or simply as a delicious accompaniment to your meals.

Estonian Carrot Bread (Porgandileib)

Preparation time: 20 minutes
Cook time: 50 minutes
Nutrition facts (per serving): 232 Cal (14g fat, 7g protein, 1.3g fiber)

Porgandileib, or Estonian carrot bread, is a deliciously moist and sweet loaf made with grated carrots, perfect for adding a touch of natural sweetness to your morning toast or afternoon snack.

Ingredients (8 servings)

2 cups all-purpose flour
1 cup carrots, grated
½ cup sugar
½ cup vegetable oil
2 large eggs
1 teaspoon baking powder
½ teaspoon baking soda
½ teaspoon salt
1 teaspoon cinnamon
½ teaspoon nutmeg
½ cup chopped walnuts or pecans (optional)

Preparation

At 350°F, preheat your oven and grease a loaf pan. In a suitable mixing bowl, mix the sugar, flour, baking powder, baking soda, salt, cinnamon, and nutmeg. Stir to mix well. In a separate bowl, whisk the grated carrots, vegetable oil, and eggs until well combined. Stir in the carrot mixture to the dry ingredients and stir until just combined. If using nuts, fold in the chopped walnuts or pecans. Pour the prepared batter into the greased loaf pan and smooth the top with a spatula.

Bake in the preheated oven for 45-50 minutes, until a toothpick inserted into the center of the bread comes out clean. Remove the carrot bread from the oven and leave it to cool in the pan for 10 minutes, then place it onto the wire rack to cool completely. Once the bread has cooled, slice and serve as desired. It can be enjoyed plain, with butter, or as a sandwich bread.

Poppy Seed Bread (Moonileib)

Preparation time: 20 minutes
Cook time: 40 minutes
Nutrition facts (per serving): 268 Cal (26g fat, 9g protein, 0.3g fiber)

Moonileib, or Estonian poppy seed bread, is a traditional bread with a nutty and slightly sweet flavor, dotted with crunchy poppy seeds, making it a delightful treat for poppy seed lovers.

Ingredients (8 servings)
Dough
2 cups all-purpose flour
½ cup sugar
1 teaspoon active dry yeast
½ teaspoon salt
½ cup milk
¼ cup unsalted butter, melted
2 large eggs
1 teaspoon vanilla extract

Poppy Seed Filling
1 cup poppy seeds
½ cup milk
¼ cup honey
¼ cup sugar
¼ cup unsalted butter
½ teaspoon vanilla extract

Preparation

In a suitable saucepan, mix the poppy seeds, milk, honey, sugar, butter, and vanilla extract For the filling. Bring to a simmer over low heat and cook for 5 minutes, stirring constantly. Remove from heat and let the filling cool to room temperature.

In a suitable mixing bowl, whisk the sugar, flour, yeast, and salt for the dough. In a separate bowl, mix the milk, melted butter, eggs, and vanilla extract. Whisk well. Stir in the dry flour mixture and stir until a dough forms. Knead this dough on a floured surface for 5-7 minutes, until it becomes smooth and elastic. Place this dough in a greased bowl, cover with a clean cloth, and let it rise in a warm place for about 1 hour, until it doubles in size. Punch down this dough and turn it out onto a floured surface. Roll it into a rectangle about ¼ inch thick. Spread the cooled poppy seed filling evenly over this dough, leaving a suitable border around the edges.

Roll up this dough tightly from the long side, jelly-roll style. Place the rolled dough seam-side down in a greased loaf pan. Cover with a clean cloth and let it rise for another 30-45 minutes. At 350°F, preheat your oven. Bake the poppy seed bread in the preheated oven for 30-35 minutes, until golden brown on top and the internal temperature reaches 190°F on an instant-read thermometer. Remove the bread from the oven and leave it to cool in the pan for 10 minutes, then place it onto the wire rack to cool completely. Once the bread has cooled, slice and serve as desired. Enjoy the delicious Estonian poppy seed bread!

Estonian Seed Bread (Seemneleib)

Preparation time: 20 minutes
Cook time: 60 minutes
Nutrition facts (per serving): 249 Cal (7g fat, 2g protein, 3g fiber)

Seemneleib, or Estonian seed bread, is a hearty and wholesome bread packed with an array of seeds, such as sunflower, flax, and sesame, providing a deliciously crunchy texture and a nutty taste.

Ingredients (8 servings)
2 cups rye flour
1 cup all-purpose flour
¼ cup sunflower seeds
¼ cup pumpkin seeds
¼ cup flaxseeds
¼ cup sesame seeds
1 teaspoon salt
1 teaspoon active dry yeast
2 cups warm water

Preparation
In a suitable mixing bowl, mix the rye flour, all-purpose flour, sunflower seeds, pumpkin seeds, flaxseeds, sesame seeds, salt, and yeast. Stir in the warm water to the dry ingredients and stir until a sticky dough forms. Cover this bowl with a clean cloth and let this dough rest for 30 minutes.

At 400°F, preheat your oven and grease a loaf pan. After this dough has rested, transfer it to the greased loaf pan and smooth the top with a wet spatula. Let this dough rise in a warm place for 30-45 minutes, until it has risen slightly and looks puffy.

Bake the seed bread in the preheated oven for 50-60 minutes, until its's golden brown on top and sounds hollow when tapped on the bottom. Remove the bread from the oven and leave it to cool in the pan for 10 minutes, then place it onto the wire rack to cool completely. Once the bread has cooled, slice and serve as desired. Enjoy the nutritious and delicious Estonian seed bread!

Estonian Pumpkin Bread (Kõrvitsaleib)

Preparation time: 20 minutes
Cook time: 60 minutes
Nutrition facts (per serving): 211 Cal (1.2g fat, 8g protein, 7g fiber)

Kõrvitsaleib, or Estonian pumpkin bread, is a moist and flavorful bread made with real pumpkin puree, warm spices, and a touch of sweetness, perfect for the autumn season.

Ingredients (8 servings)
2 cups all-purpose flour
1 cup sugar
1 teaspoon baking powder
½ teaspoon baking soda
½ teaspoon salt
1 teaspoon cinnamon
½ teaspoon nutmeg
½ teaspoon ginger
¼ teaspoon cloves
2 large eggs
1 cup pumpkin puree
½ cup vegetable oil
¼ cup milk
1 teaspoon vanilla extract

Preparation

At 350°F, preheat your oven and grease a 9x5-inch loaf pan. In a suitable mixing bowl, whisk the sugar, flour, baking powder, baking soda, salt, cinnamon, nutmeg, ginger, and cloves. In a separate bowl, beat the eggs, then stir in the pumpkin puree, vegetable oil, milk, and vanilla extract. Stir until well combined. Stir in the dry flour mixture and stir until just combined. Do not overmix. Pour the prepared batter into the greased loaf pan and smooth the top with a spatula. Bake in the preheated oven for 50-60 minutes, until a toothpick inserted into the center of the bread comes out clean. Remove the pumpkin bread from the oven and leave it to cool in the pan for 10 minutes, then place it onto the wire rack to cool completely. Once the bread has cooled, slice and serve as desired. Enjoy the delicious and moist Estonian pumpkin bread!

Estonian Oat Bread (Kaeraleib)

Preparation time: 20 minutes
Cook time: 35 minutes
Nutrition facts (per serving): 211 Cal (1.2g fat, 8g protein, 7g fiber)

Kaeraleib, or Estonian oat bread, is a wholesome and nutritious bread made with hearty oats, creating a rustic and delicious loaf that's a staple in Estonian cuisine.

Ingredients (12 servings)
2 cups rolled oats
2 cups boiling water
2 tablespoons butter
2 tablespoons molasses or honey
2 teaspoons salt
2 teaspoons active dry yeast
4 cups all-purpose flour
Extra oats, for garnish

Preparation
Place the rolled oats in a suitable mixing bowl and pour boiling water over them. Stir in the butter, molasses or honey, and salt. Let this mixture cool to lukewarm. Drizzle the yeast over the oat mixture and stir until dissolved. Stir in the flour gradually, mixing well after each addition, until a soft dough forms. Turn this dough out onto a floured surface and knead for about 5-7 minutes, until this dough is smooth and elastic.

Place this dough back into the mixing bowl and cover with a clean towel. Let it rise in a warm, draft-free place for about 1 hour, until it has doubled in size. At 375°F, preheat your oven and grease a 9x5-inch loaf pan. Punch down this dough and turn it out onto a lightly floured surface. Shape it into a loaf and place it into the prepared loaf pan. Drizzle the top with extra oats for garnish. Let this dough rise in the pan for about 15-20 minutes, until it has risen slightly. Bake in the preheated oven for 30-35 minutes, until the bread is golden brown and sounds hollow when tapped on the bottom.

Remove the oat bread from the oven and leave it to cool in the pan for 10 minutes, then place it onto the wire rack to cool completely. Once the bread has cooled, slice and serve, as desired. Enjoy the hearty and flavorful Estonian oat bread!

Martsipan
(Marzipan)

Preparation time: 15 minutes
Nutrition facts (per serving): 162 Cal (2.8g fat, 7.5g protein, 1g fiber)

Marzipan, a confectionery made from ground almonds and sugar, is a delicately sweet and smooth treat that's often shaped into intricate designs and used for decorating cakes and pastries, adding an artistic touch to culinary creations.

Ingredients (8 servings)
2 cups almond flour or blanched almonds
2 cups sugar, powdered
½ teaspoon almond extract
½ teaspoon rosewater, optional
Food coloring (optional)
Sugar, granulated or powdered, for dusting

Preparation
If using whole almonds, blanch them by placing them in boiling water for a few minutes, then draining and removing the skins. Allow them to dry completely. In a food processor, mix the almond flour or blanched almonds with powdered sugar. Pulse until well combined and this mixture has a fine texture. Stir in the almond extract and rosewater (if using) to this mixture and pulse again until this mixture starts to come together and forms a dough-like consistency. If desired, you can add food

coloring to this mixture to achieve the desired color. Pulse until the color is evenly distributed.

Turn out the marzipan mixture onto a clean work surface and knead it with your hands until it forms a smooth ball of dough. If the marzipan is too sticky, you can dust your hands and work surface with a little powdered sugar or granulated sugar to help with handling. Once the marzipan is smooth and pliable, you can shape it into desired forms. It can be rolled out and cut into shapes, formed into balls, or shaped into various decorations. If not using immediately, wrap the marzipan tightly in plastic wrap and store it in an airtight container in the refrigerator for up to 2 weeks. Marzipan can be used to cover cakes, create decorative figures, or simply enjoy it as a sweet treat on its own. Enjoy your homemade marzipan!

Estonian Sweet Bun (Saiake)

Preparation time: 20 minutes
Cook time: 27 minutes
Nutrition facts (per serving): 212 Cal (9g fat, 7g protein, 0.5g fiber)

Saiake, an Estonian sweet bun, is a delectable treat known for its soft and fluffy texture, often enjoyed with a cup of coffee or tea as a delightful indulgence.

Ingredients (8 servings)
Dough
1 lb. all-purpose flour
1 teaspoon active dry yeast
3 ½ oz. sugar
1 cup milk
3 ½ oz. butter, melted
1 teaspoon salt
1 teaspoon cardamom

Filling
3 ½ oz. butter, softened
3 ½ oz. sugar
1 teaspoon vanilla extract

Glaze
1 egg, beaten
Pearl sugar, for sprinkling (optional)

Preparation

In a suitable mixing bowl, mix the flour, yeast, sugar, salt, and cardamom. Stir to mix well. In a saucepan, heat the milk until warm, then stir in the melted butter. Stir to combine. Stir in the milk mixture to the dry ingredients in the mixing bowl, and mix until a soft dough forms. Turn this dough out onto a floured surface and knead for about 5-7 minutes, until it becomes smooth and elastic. Place this dough back into the mixing bowl, cover with a clean towel, and let it rise in a warm place for about 1 hour, until it has doubled in size.

At 350°F, preheat your oven and line a baking sheet with parchment paper. Punch down the risen dough and turn it out onto a floured surface. Divide it into small pieces and shape each piece into a suitable bun.

In a suitable bowl, mix together the softened butter, sugar, and vanilla extract to make the filling. Flatten each bun with your fingers, and place a suitable dollop of the filling in the center of each bun. Fold the edges of this dough over the filling and pinch to seal, forming a ball-shaped bun. Place the filled buns onto the prepared baking sheet, leaving some space between them. Brush the buns with beaten egg, and drizzle with pearl sugar (if using).

Bake the buns in the preheated oven for 15-20 minutes, until they turn golden brown on top. Remove the buns from the oven and let them cool on the baking sheet for a few minutes, then transfer them to a wire rack to cool completely. Once the buns have cooled, serve and enjoy your delicious Estonian sweet buns!

Traditional Estonian Bread (Kama Leib)

Preparation time: 20 minutes
Cook time: 52 minutes
Nutrition facts (per serving): 270 Cal (12g fat, 4g protein, 6 g fiber)

Kama leib, a traditional Estonian bread made with kama flour, is a hearty and wholesome loaf that's beloved for its unique flavor and nutritious ingredients.

Ingredients (8 servings)
1 lb. rye flour
1 lb. wheat flour
9 oz. kama powder (Estonian roasted grain powder)
1 tablespoon salt
1 tablespoon sugar
1 tablespoon active dry yeast
2 cups warm water

Preparation
In a suitable mixing bowl, mix the rye flour, wheat flour, kama powder, salt, sugar, and active dry yeast. Stir to mix well. Gradually stir in the warm water to the dry ingredients while mixing, until a dough forms. You may need to adjust the amount of water slightly to achieve the right consistency. Turn this dough out onto a floured surface and knead for about 5-7 minutes, until it becomes smooth and elastic. Place this dough

back into the mixing bowl, cover with a clean towel, and let it rise in a warm place for about 1 hour, until it has doubled in size.

At 400°F, preheat your oven and line a loaf pan with parchment paper. Punch down the risen dough and turn it out onto a floured surface. Shape it into a loaf and place it into the prepared loaf pan. Cover the loaf pan with a clean towel and let this dough rise for another 30 minutes. Bake the kama bread in the preheated oven for 40-45 minutes, until golden brown on top and sounds hollow when tapped on the bottom.

Remove the bread from the oven and leave it to cool in the loaf pan for a few minutes, then place it onto the wire rack to cool completely. Once the kama bread has cooled, slice and serve as desired. It's traditionally enjoyed with butter, cheese, or other toppings.

Blueberry Porridge (Mustikapuder)

Preparation time: 20 minutes
Cook time: 14 minutes
Nutrition facts (per serving): 249 Cal (0g fat, 1.1g protein, 0g fiber)

Mustikapuder, or Estonian Blueberry Porridge, is a classic Estonian dessert that's often enjoyed for breakfast or as a comforting dessert. Made with fresh or frozen blueberries, this creamy and delicious porridge is typically served warm and can be easily prepared with just a few simple ingredients.

Ingredients (2 servings)
1 cup fresh or frozen blueberries
1 cup water
½ cup rolled oats
½ cup milk
2 tablespoons sugar
¼ teaspoon salt
½ teaspoon vanilla extract

Preparation
In a suitable saucepan, mix the blueberries and water. Bring to a boil over medium heat and then reduce its heat to low. Simmer for about 5-7 minutes, until the blueberries have softened and released their juices. Stir in the rolled oats, milk, sugar, salt, and vanilla extract. Cook over low heat, stirring frequently, for about 5-7 minutes, until the oats have

absorbed the liquid and the porridge has thickened to your desired consistency. Remove from heat and let the porridge cool for a few minutes before serving. Serve the Mustikapuder warm in bowls or dessert dishes. You can garnish with additional blueberries, a drizzle of sugar, or a dollop of whipped cream, if desired. Enjoy the warm and comforting flavors of Mustikapuder, a traditional Estonian blueberry porridge. It's a simple and delicious dessert that is perfect for breakfast or a sweet treat any time of the day!

Black Rye Bread (Rukkileib)

Preparation time: 20 minutes
Cook time: 60 minutes
Nutrition facts (per serving): 120 Cal (3.6gfat, 4.2g protein, 0.6g fiber)

Rukkileib, a staple in Estonian cuisine, is a dense and flavorful black rye bread with a distinctive tangy taste and a hearty texture, often enjoyed with various toppings as a wholesome and satisfying meal.

Ingredients (8 servings)
2 cups rye flour
2 cups whole wheat flour
½ cup all-purpose flour
2 ½ cups buttermilk
½ cup molasses
¼ cup dark corn syrup
1 teaspoon salt
1 teaspoon baking soda
2 tablespoons cocoa powder
½ cup sunflower seeds, optional

Preparation
In a suitable mixing bowl, whisk the rye flour, whole wheat flour, and all-purpose flour. In a separate bowl, mix the buttermilk, molasses, and dark corn syrup. Mix well. Stir in the buttermilk mixture to the dry ingredients

and stir until a thick, sticky dough forms. Cover this bowl with a clean towel or plastic wrap and let it sit at room temperature for 12-24 hours to allow this dough to ferment and develop flavor.

After the fermentation period, at 350°F, preheat your oven. Grease a 9x5-inch loaf pan and set aside. Stir the salt, baking soda, and cocoa powder into the fermented dough until well combined. If desired, stir in sunflower seeds or other add-ins at this point. Transfer this dough to the prepared loaf pan and smooth the top with a spatula. Bake the bread in the preheated oven for 50-60 minutes until a toothpick inserted into the center comes out clean. Remove the bread from the oven and leave it to cool in the pan for 10 minutes, then place it onto the wire rack to cool completely. Once the bread is completely cooled, you can slice it and enjoy your homemade black rye bread!

Estonian Porridge

Preparation time: 10 minutes
Cook time: 7 minutes
Nutrition facts (per serving): 235 Cal (3.8g fat, 6.8g protein, 1.4g fiber)

Estonian Porridge can be made with different types of grains, such as barley, rice, or semolina, depending on your preference. You can also adjust the sweetness and consistency of the porridge to your liking by adding more or less sugar, milk, or water. It's a versatile dish that can be enjoyed for breakfast, a snack, or even as a dessert.

Ingredients (2 servings)
1 cup rolled oats
2 cups water
¼ teaspoon salt
2 cups milk
1 tablespoon butter
Berries, nuts, seeds, honey, or jam, for topping

Preparation
In a suitable saucepan, mix the rolled oats, water, and salt. Bring to a boil over medium heat. Reduce the heat to low and simmer for about 5 minutes, stirring occasionally, until the oats have absorbed most of the liquid and have softened. Stir in the milk to the saucepan and continue to simmer for another 5-7 minutes, stirring frequently, until the porridge reaches your desired consistency. If it becomes too thick, you can add more milk to adjust the consistency. Remove the saucepan from the heat

and stir in the butter until melted. Serve the porridge hot in bowls and add your desired toppings, such as berries, nuts, seeds, honey, or jam. Enjoy your warm and comforting Estonian Porridge!

Mashed Eggs
(Munavõi)

Preparation time: 15 minutes
Nutrition facts (per serving): 225 Cal (17g fat, 13g protein, 1.2g fiber)

Estonian Eggs, also known as "Munavõi," is a traditional Estonian dish made with hard-boiled eggs and butter. It's often served as a spread on bread or crackers, and it's a popular dish during festive occasions like Easter.

Ingredients (2 servings)
4 hard-boiled eggs
½ cup unsalted butter, at room temperature
½ teaspoon salt
¼ teaspoon black pepper
Fresh chives, dill, or parsley, for garnish

Preparation
Peel the hard-boiled eggs and chop them into small pieces. In a suitable mixing bowl, stir in the softened butter, black pepper, and salt. Mix well until combined. Stir the chopped hard-boiled in bowl with the butter mixture. Use a fork or a potato masher to mash the eggs and butter together until creamy and well combined. Taste and adjust the seasoning with more salt or pepper, if desired. Transfer the Estonian Eggs to a serving dish and garnish with fresh chives, dill, or parsley, if desired. Serve the Munavõi as a spread on bread or crackers, and enjoy!

Estonian Sausage (Eesti Vorst)

Preparation time: 10 minutes
Cook time: 24 minutes
Nutrition facts (per serving): 232 Cal (14g fat, 10g protein, 1.3g fiber)

Estonian sausage, known as "Eesti Vorst" is a popular traditional dish in Estonia. It's a flavorful sausage made with minced meat and spices, often served grilled or pan-fried.

Ingredients (4 servings)
1 lb. ground pork or beef
½ lb. pork fatback, finely diced
1 small onion, finely minced
2 cloves garlic, minced
1 teaspoon salt
½ teaspoon black pepper
½ teaspoon ground allspice
½ teaspoon ground coriander
½ teaspoon ground paprika
¼ teaspoon ground nutmeg
¼ teaspoon ground cloves
Natural sausage casings, to taste
Cooking oil, if pan-frying

Preparation

In a suitable mixing bowl, mix the ground pork or beef with the diced pork fatback, minced onion, minced garlic, salt, black pepper, allspice, coriander, paprika, nutmeg, and cloves. Mix well until all the ingredients are thoroughly combined. If using natural sausage casings, prepare them according to the manufacturer's instructions. Soak them in warm water for about 30 minutes to soften them before using. Stuff the meat mixture into the sausage casings using a sausage stuffer or your hands. Twist the sausages at regular intervals to form links. If you prefer not to use casings, you can shape the sausage mixture into patties or logs by hand. If grilling, preheat your grill to medium-high heat.

Grill the sausages for about 10-12 minutes, occasionally turning, until they are cooked through and have a nicely browned exterior. If pan-frying, heat a pan over medium heat and add a little cooking oil. Pan-fry the sausages for about 10-12 minutes, occasionally turning, until they are cooked through and have a golden-brown crust. Once cooked, transfer the Estonian sausages to a serving platter and let them rest for a few minutes before serving. Serve the Estonian sausages hot with your favorite side dishes, such as sauerkraut, potatoes, or a side of mustard for dipping.

Estonian Omelet

Preparation time: 10 minutes
Cook time: 5 minutes
Nutrition facts (per serving): 218 Cal (2g fat, 24.5g protein, 3.2g fiber)

Estonian omelet, also known as "Omlett," is a simple and delicious dish made with eggs, milk, and various fillings. It's a popular breakfast or brunch option in Estonia and can be customized with your favorite ingredients.

Ingredients (4 servings)
4 large eggs
¼ cup milk
½ teaspoon salt
¼ teaspoon black pepper
1 tablespoon butter or cooking oil
½ cup shredded cheese (cheddar, Swiss or gouda)
½ cup vegetables (bell peppers, onions, mushrooms or tomatoes), chopped
Chives, parsley, or dill, for garnish

Preparation
In a suitable mixing bowl, whisk the eggs, milk, black pepper, and salt until well combined. Heat a non-stick skillet over medium heat and melt the butter or heat the cooking oil. Stir in the chopped vegetables to the skillet and cook for 2-3 minutes until they're slightly softened. Pour the egg mixture over the vegetables in the skillet and let it cook without stirring for a few minutes until the edges are set, and the center is still

slightly jiggly. Drizzle the shredded cheese evenly over the omelet. Carefully fold the omelet in half using a spatula, covering the fillings with the other half of the omelet. Cook for another 1-2 minutes until the cheese is melted and the omelet is cooked through. Slide the Estonian omelet onto a serving plate and garnish with fresh herbs, if desired. Cut the omelet into wedges and serve it hot as a delicious and satisfying breakfast or brunch dish.

Potato Pancakes

Preparation time: 15 minutes
Cook time: 6 minutes
Nutrition facts (per serving): 148 Cal (1g fat, 4.5g protein, 3.1g fiber)

The crispy potato pancakes are one of the special meals of the Estonian breakfast, and you can serve them with creamy dips and sauce.

Ingredients (6 servings)
5 potatoes white, medium, peeled
1 onion, medium
1 egg
3 tablespoons flour
Sea salt, to taste
Black pepper, to taste

Preparation
Grate the potatoes in the food processor and add the shreds to a bowl. Add egg, flour, black pepper, salt, and chopped onion. Mix well using a fork until it makes a rough dough. Place an iron pan over medium heat and add coconut oil to heat. Add ¼ of the potato batter to the pan and press it into a pancake. Cook for 2-3 minutes until golden brown from both sides. Continue making more pancakes using the potato mixture. Serve.

Estonian Modern Porridge (Hommikupuder)

Preparation time: 10 minutes
Cook time: 7 minutes
Nutrition facts (per serving): 148 Cal (5.5g fat, 5.8g protein, 0.5g fiber)

Estonian morning porridge, also known as "Hommikupuder" or "Kaerahelbepuder" is a popular breakfast dish in Estonia. It's a simple and nutritious porridge made with rolled oats, water, or milk and sometimes flavored with cinnamon, cardamom, or other spices.

Ingredients (2 servings)
1 cup rolled oats
2 cups water or milk (or a combination of both)
¼ teaspoon salt
Fresh or dried fruits (berries, apples, or raisins), for topping
Nuts, seeds, honey, maple syrup, for topping

Preparation
In a saucepan, mix the rolled oats, water or milk, and salt. Stir well to combine. Place the saucepan over medium heat and bring this mixture to a boil, stirring occasionally. Reduce the heat to low and simmer the porridge, occasionally stirring, for about 5-7 minutes until it reaches your desired consistency. If using water, it may take slightly longer to cook compared to using milk.

Remove the saucepan from the heat and let the porridge sit for a minute or two to thicken. Serve the Estonian morning porridge hot in bowls. Customize the porridge with your favorite toppings, such as fresh or dried fruits, nuts, seeds, honey, maple syrup, or other sweeteners, according to your preferences. Stir in the toppings gently before enjoying your warm and comforting bowl of Estonian morning porridge.

Estonian vegetable omelet (Juurviljaomlett)

Preparation time: 20 minutes
Cook time: 12 minutes
Nutrition facts (per serving): 241 Cal (3.3g fat, 9.8g protein, 1.2g fiber)

Juurviljaomlett, an Estonian vegetable omelet, is a nutritious and flavorful dish made with a variety of locally sourced vegetables, eggs, and herbs, cooked to perfection for a wholesome and delicious meal that is a popular choice for breakfast or brunch in Estonian cuisine.

Ingredients (2 servings)
4 large eggs
¼ cup milk
½ cup grated cheese (cheddar or Gouda)
1 small onion, finely chopped
1 small carrot, peeled and grated
1 small zucchini, grated
1 small bell pepper, finely chopped
2 tablespoons butter
Black pepper, to taste
Salt, to taste
Fresh parsley, for garnish

Preparation

In a suitable bowl, whisk the eggs and milk until well combined. Stir in the grated cheese. Heat a non-stick skillet over medium heat and melt the butter. Stir in the chopped onion, grated carrot, grated zucchini, and chopped bell pepper in the skillet. Sauté for 3-4 minutes, until the vegetables are softened. Pour the egg mixture over the sautéed vegetables in the skillet. Cook for 4-5 minutes, until the edges, are set and the center is slightly jiggly. Use a spatula to gently lift the edges of the Omelet and tilt the skillet to allow the uncooked eggs to flow underneath.

Once it's mostly set, carefully flip it over using a suitable spatula or by inverting it onto a plate and sliding it back into the skillet. Cook for another 2-3 minutes, until the Omelet is fully set and lightly golden brown. Season with black pepper and salt to taste. Slide the Omelet onto a serving plate, cut it into wedges, and garnish with fresh parsley, if desired. Serve hot, and enjoy your delicious Estonian Vegetable Omelet!

Estonian Barley Porridge (Oderpuder)

Preparation time: 15 minutes
Cook time: 40 minutes
Nutrition facts (per serving): 139 Cal (11.5g fat, 7.1g protein, 0g fiber)

Estonian barley porridge, also known as "Oderpuder" or "Pearl Barley Porridge," is a traditional dish in Estonia that is often served as a comforting and hearty breakfast or a warming meal during colder months. It's made with pearl barley, water, or broth, and sometimes flavored with onions, carrots, and other ingredients.

Ingredients (2 servings)

1 cup pearl barley
4 cups water or broth (chicken, vegetable, or beef)
½ teaspoon salt
1 medium onion, finely chopped (optional)
1 medium carrot, grated (optional)
2 tablespoons butter or cooking oil (optional)
Fresh parsley or dill, for garnish (optional)

Preparation

Rinse the pearl barley under cold water in a fine-mesh strainer to remove any impurities. In a suitable saucepan, mix the rinsed pearl barley, water or broth, and salt. If using, stir in the finely chopped onion and grated carrot for extra flavor. Place the saucepan over medium heat and bring this mixture to a boil. Reduce the heat to low and let the barley simmer, covered, for about 30-40 minutes until it is tender. Stir occasionally to prevent sticking to the bottom of the pan.

If using, add butter or cooking oil to the cooked barley and stir well to incorporate. Taste the barley porridge and adjust the seasoning with more salt or other spices according to your preferences. Remove the saucepan from the heat and let the barley porridge sit for a few minutes to thicken. Serve the Estonian barley porridge hot in bowls, garnished with fresh parsley or dill, if desired. Enjoy your warm and comforting bowl of Estonian barley porridge as a delicious and filling breakfast or a satisfying meal.

Snacks

Broad Beans Fritters
(Hõrgud Kõrtpoolakesed)

Preparation time: 10 minutes
Cook time: 10 minutes
Nutrition facts (per serving): 209 Cal (4.7g fat, 7.8g protein, 2g fiber)

Broad bean fritters, also known as "Hõrgud Kõrtpoolakesed" in Estonian cuisine, are a delicious and crispy snack made with broad beans or fava beans. They're typically seasoned with herbs and spices and then fried until golden brown.

Ingredients (4 servings)
1 cup broad beans or fava beans, shelled
1 small onion, finely chopped
2 cloves garlic, minced
½ cup all-purpose flour
½ teaspoon baking powder
1 teaspoon dried herbs (parsley, dill, or thyme)
½ teaspoon salt
¼ teaspoon black pepper
1 large egg
Oil, for frying

Preparation
In a suitable bowl, mix the shelled broad beans, finely chopped onion, minced garlic, all-purpose flour, baking powder, dried herbs, black pepper, and salt. Stir well to combine. Stir in the egg to this mixture and

mix until the ingredients are well incorporated. Heat about ½ inch of oil in a frying pan over medium-high heat. Drop spoonfuls of the broad bean mixture into the hot oil and flatten slightly with the back of a spoon to form fritters. Fry the fritters for about 2-3 minutes per side until they are golden brown and crispy.

Using a slotted spoon, transfer the fried fritters to a paper towel-lined plate to drain any excess oil. Repeat the process with the remaining broad bean mixture, adding more oil to the pan as needed. Serve the broad beans fritters hot as a tasty appetizer, snack, or side dish. Enjoy your crispy and flavorful broad bean fritters with your favorite dipping sauce, such as yogurt sauce, aioli, or sour cream, if desired.

Estonian Curd Snack (Kohupiimakreem)

Preparation time: 10 minutes
Nutrition facts (per serving): 206 Cal (14.6g fat, 7.7g protein, 1.2g fiber)

Estonian curd snack, also known as "Kohupiimakreem" in Estonian cuisine, is a popular dessert or snack made with curd cheese or cottage cheese, sugar, and typically flavored with vanilla or other flavorings. It's often served chilled and can be enjoyed on its own or topped with fruits or berries.

Ingredients (4 servings)

2 cups curd cheese or cottage cheese
½ cup sugar
1 teaspoon vanilla extract or other flavorings (optional)
Fresh fruits or berries (strawberries, blueberries, or raspberries), for topping
Fresh mint leaves, for garnish (optional)

Preparation

In a suitable mixing bowl, mix the curd cheese or cottage cheese, sugar, vanilla extract, or other flavorings (if using). Stir well to combine. Taste this mixture and adjust the sweetness to your preference by adding more sugar if desired. Spoon the curd cheese mixture into serving bowls or glasses. Chill the curd snack in the refrigerator for at least 1 hour to allow the flavors to meld and this mixture to set. Just before serving, top the curd snack with fresh fruits or berries of your choice. Garnish with fresh mint leaves, if desired, for added freshness and color. Serve the Estonian curd snack chilled and enjoy it as a delicious and refreshing dessert or snack.

Estonian Semla (Vastlakukkel)

Preparation time: 10 minutes
Cook time: 15 minutes
Nutrition facts (per serving): 207 Cal (2.1g fat, 8.3g protein, 1.7g fiber)

Estonian Semla, also known as "Vastlakukkel" in Estonian cuisine, is a traditional sweet bun typically associated with Shrove Tuesday or "Vastlapäev" in Estonia. It's a delicious treat made with a cardamom-flavored bun filled with whipped cream and almond paste and often dusted with powdered sugar on top.

Ingredients (8 servings)
Bun
2 cups all-purpose flour
¼ cup sugar, granulated
½ teaspoon salt
1 teaspoon active dry yeast
½ cup milk
¼ cup unsalted butter, melted
1 large egg
1 teaspoon ground cardamom
Powdered sugar, for dusting

Almond Paste Filling
½ cup ground almonds

½ cup sugar, powdered
1 tablespoon unsalted butter, softened
½ teaspoon almond extract
¼ cup milk

Whipped Cream Filling
1 cup heavy cream
2 tablespoons powdered sugar
1 teaspoon vanilla extract

Preparation
Bun
In a suitable mixing bowl, whisk the sugar, flour, salt, and active dry yeast. In a suitable saucepan, heat the milk until warm (about 110°F/43°C). Stir in the warm milk, melted butter, egg, and ground cardamom to the dry ingredients. Stir well to form a dough. Turn this dough out onto a floured surface and knead for about 5-7 minutes until this dough is smooth and elastic. Place this dough back into the mixing bowl, cover it with a clean towel, and let it rise in a warm place for about 1 hour until it has doubled in size.

At 350°F, preheat your oven and line a baking sheet with parchment paper. Punch down the risen dough and divide it into 10-12 equal portions. Shape each portion into a suitable round bun and place it on the prepared baking sheet. Bake the buns in the preheated oven for 12-15 minutes until they are golden brown on top. Remove the buns from the oven and let them cool completely on a wire rack.

Almond Paste Filling

In a suitable mixing bowl, mix the ground almonds, powdered sugar, softened butter, and almond extract. Stir well to form a thick paste. Add the milk gradually, as needed, until the almond paste reaches a spreadable consistency.

Whipped Cream Filling

In a separate mixing bowl, whip the heavy cream, powdered sugar, and vanilla extract until stiff peaks form. Assembly: Once the buns are completely cooled, cut off the top of each bun and set the tops aside. Scoop out a suitable portion of the bun's center to create a cavity. For the fillings: Fill the cavity with a spoonful of almond paste filling. Pipe or spoon a generous amount of whipped cream on top of the almond paste filling. Place the reserved bun tops back on top of the whipped cream. Dust the buns with powdered sugar on top for decoration. Serve the Estonian Semla as a delicious and traditional treat for Shrove Tuesday or any time of the year!

Estonian Sprat Sandwich (Sprotivõileib)

Preparation time: 15 minutes
Nutrition facts (per serving): 255 Cal (5g fat, 18.5g protein, 1.5g fiber)

Estonian Sprat Sandwich, also known as "Sprotivõileib" in Estonian cuisine, is a popular open-faced sandwich that features sprats, a type of small fish commonly found in the Baltic Sea. It's a simple and tasty sandwich that's often enjoyed as a quick and satisfying snack.

Ingredients (4 servings)

4 sliced rye bread or any other bread
4 canned sprats in oil
2 tablespoons softened butter
1 red onion, thinly sliced
1 tablespoon fresh dill, chopped
Lemon wedges, for serving

Preparation

Toast or lightly butter the slices of bread. Drain the canned sprats, reserving the oil. Spread a thin layer of softened butter on each slice of bread. Arrange a few sprats on top of the buttered bread slices, making sure to leave some space between the fish. Top the sprats with thinly sliced red onion and a drizzle of chopped fresh dill. Drizzle a little bit of the reserved oil from the canned sprats over the top for added flavor. Serve the Sprat Sandwiches with lemon wedges on the side for squeezing over the top before eating. Enjoy the Estonian Sprat Sandwiches as a tasty and satisfying snack or appetizer!

Potato Chips
(Kartulikrõpsud)

Preparation time: 10 minutes
Cook time: 5 minutes
Nutrition facts (per serving): 275 Cal (7g fat, 6g protein, 2g fiber)

Kartulikrõpsud, Estonian potato chips, are crispy and savory snacks made from locally grown potatoes, offering a deliciously addictive crunch and a taste of Estonia's culinary heritage in every bite.

Ingredients (8 servings)
4 medium potatoes
Salt, to taste
Cooking oil, for frying

Preparation
Wash and peel the potatoes. Using a sharp knife or a Mandoline slicer, thinly slice the potatoes into uniform rounds. Place the potato slices in a suitable bowl of cold water and let them soak for about 10 minutes to remove excess starch. Drain the potato slices and pat them dry with a clean kitchen towel or paper towels.

In a deep frying pan or a deep fryer, heat the cooking oil to about 180°C (350°F). Carefully stir in the potato slices to the hot oil in small batches, without overcrowding the pan. Fry the potato slices until they are golden brown and crispy, turning occasionally to ensure even frying. Using a slotted spoon, remove the fried potato chips from the oil and place them on paper towels to drain off excess oil. Immediately liberally season the hot potato chips liberally with salt while they are still greasy, to ensure that the salt sticks to the chips. Repeat the frying process with the remaining potato slices. Allow the potato chips to cool completely before serving. Store the Estonian potato chips in an airtight container to maintain their crispiness.

Onion Rings
(Sibulakrõpsud)

Preparation time: 10 minutes
Cook time: 10 minutes
Nutrition facts (per serving): 207 Cal (14g fat, 7g protein, 1g fiber)

Sibulakrõpsud, Estonian onion rings, are crispy and flavorful snacks made from thinly sliced onions, coated in a seasoned batter and deep-fried to golden perfection, offering a deliciously addictive taste of Estonia's culinary delights.

Ingredients (4 servings)
2 large onions
1 cup all-purpose flour
1 teaspoon baking powder
½ teaspoon salt
¼ teaspoon black pepper
¼ teaspoon paprika
¼ teaspoon garlic powder
¼ teaspoon onion powder
½ cup cold water
Cooking oil, for frying

Preparation
Peel the onions and cut them into thin slices, separating the rings. In a suitable mixing bowl, whisk the flour, baking powder, salt, black pepper, paprika, garlic powder, and onion powder. Gradually stir in the cold

water to the dry ingredients, whisking until a smooth batter is formed. In a deep frying pan or a deep fryer, heat the cooking oil to about 180°C (350°F). Dip the onion rings into the prepared batter, allowing any excess batter to drain off, and carefully place them in the hot oil, a few at a time. Fry the onion rings until they are golden brown and crispy, turning occasionally to ensure even frying. Using a slotted spoon, remove the fried onion rings from the oil and place them on paper towels to drain off excess oil. Repeat the frying process with the remaining onion rings. Allow the Estonian onion rings to cool slightly before serving. Serve the onion rings as a delicious and crispy snack or appetizer.

Roasted Grain Snack (Kama)

Preparation time: 10 minutes
Cook time: 25 minutes
Nutrition facts (per serving): 132 Cal (4g fat, 4g protein, 1.3g fiber)

Kama is a traditional Estonian food made from roasted grains and often used in various recipes. This recipe is for making kama as a snack, but you can also find other recipes that use kama as an ingredient in Estonian cuisine.

Ingredients (8 servings)
1 cup whole wheat flour
1 cup rye flour
½ cup barley flour
½ cup oat flour
½ cup buckwheat flour
½ cup flaxseed meal
½ cup sugar, powdered
½ cup cocoa powder
½ teaspoon salt
½ cup unsalted butter, melted
½ cup honey

Preparation
At 350°F, preheat your oven and line a baking sheet with parchment paper. In a suitable mixing bowl, whisk the whole wheat flour, rye flour,

barley flour, oat flour, buckwheat flour, flaxseed meal, powdered sugar, cocoa powder, and salt. Stir in the melted butter and honey to the dry ingredients and mix well until a crumbly dough forms. Spread this dough evenly onto the prepared baking sheet and press it down with a spatula or your hands to compact it. Bake this dough in the preheated oven for 20-25 minutes until it is lightly golden brown. Remove the baked dough from the oven and leave it to cool completely on the baking sheet. Once cooled, break the baked dough into small pieces or crumble it into a suitable bowl to form a crunchy and nutritious Estonian roasted grain snack. Serve the kama snack as a tasty and wholesome treat, perfect for enjoying on its own or as a topping for yogurt, porridge, or other desserts.

Wild Garlic Chips (Karulauguviilud)

Preparation time: 15 minutes
Cook time: 10 minutes
Nutrition facts (per serving): 132 Cal (4g fat, 2g protein, 1.3g fiber)

Karulauguviilud, or wild garlic chips, are a popular Estonian snack made from wild garlic leaves. They are typically enjoyed during the spring season when wild garlic is abundant. Wild garlic has a pungent and garlicky flavor that adds a unique twist to these crispy chips.

Ingredients (4 servings)
1 bunch of wild garlic leaves
1 cup all-purpose flour
½ teaspoon salt
¼ teaspoon black pepper
¼ teaspoon paprika
¼ teaspoon garlic powder
¼ teaspoon onion powder
½ cup cold water
Vegetable oil, for frying

Preparation
Wash and dry the wild garlic leaves thoroughly, then trim off any tough stems. In a suitable mixing bowl, whisk the flour, salt, black pepper, paprika, garlic powder, and onion powder. Gradually stir in the cold water to the dry ingredients, whisking continuously, until a thick batter

is formed. Heat vegetable oil in a deep frying pan or deep fryer to a temperature of around 350°F (180°C).

Dip each wild garlic leaf into the prepared batter, coating it evenly on both sides. Carefully place the coated wild garlic leaves into the hot oil, frying them in batches, for about 1-2 minutes per side until they are golden brown and crispy. Use a slotted spoon or a wire mesh strainer to transfer the fried wild garlic chips to a paper towel-lined plate to drain any excess oil. Repeat the frying process with the remaining wild garlic leaves and batter. Once all the wild garlic chips are fried and drained, let them cool slightly before serving as a delicious Estonian wild garlic snack. Enjoy the crispy and flavorful wild garlic chips on their own, or as a unique and tasty accompaniment to other dishes.

Canned Moose Meat (Põdralihakonserv)

Preparation time: 10 minutes
Cook time: 2 hours
Nutrition facts (per serving): 344 Cal (19g fat, 7g protein, 3.3g fiber)

Põdralihakonserv, or Estonian canned moose meat, is a traditional dish in Estonia, where game meat is commonly consumed. This recipe can also be adapted to use other types of game meat, such as venison or elk, or even beef as a substitute. The pressure canning process ensures proper preservation and shelf-stability of the canned meat for long-term storage. Proper canning techniques and food safety guidelines should be followed to ensure safe preservation of the meat.

Ingredients (2 servings)
1 lb. moose meat (can be substituted with beef or venison)
1 onion, finely chopped
2 cloves of garlic, minced
2 tablespoons vegetable oil
1 tablespoon all-purpose flour
1 tablespoon tomato paste
1 bay leaf
1 teaspoon salt
½ teaspoon black pepper
½ teaspoon paprika
¼ teaspoon ground allspice
¼ teaspoon ground nutmeg

1 cup beef or vegetable broth
½ cup red wine (optional)

Preparation

Cut the moose meat into small cubes and season with black pepper and salt. Heat the vegetable oil in a suitable pot or Dutch oven over medium-high heat. Stir in the moose meat and sear until browned on all sides. Remove the meat from the pot and set aside. In the same pot, stir in the chopped onion and minced garlic. Sauté until softened and lightly browned. Stir in the flour and tomato paste, and cook for 1-2 minutes until well combined.

Gradually stir in the beef or vegetable broth and red wine (if using), stirring constantly to avoid lumps. Stir in the bay leaf, paprika, allspice, nutmeg, and seared moose meat back to the pot. Stir to combine. Bring this mixture to a boil, then reduce the heat to low and let it simmer for about 1-2 hours, until the moose meat is tender and easily falls apart. Taste and adjust seasoning with additional black pepper and salt, if needed. Once the meat is cooked and tender, remove the bay leaf and discard. Allow the canned moose meat to cool to room temperature.

Transfer the meat and sauce to clean, sterilized jars, leaving about ½ inch of headspace at the top. Seal the jars with lids and process in a pressure canner according to the manufacturer's instructions for meat products. Allow the jars to cool completely before storing in a cool, dark place for long-term storage. The canned moose meat can be used as a delicious and convenient protein source for sandwiches, stews, soups, or other recipes.

Estonian herring slices (Kiluviilud)

Preparation time: 10 minutes
Nutrition facts (per serving): 271 Cal (3g fat, 22g protein, 4g fiber)

Kiluviilud, or Estonian herring slices, are a popular traditional dish in Estonia, especially during festive occasions and holiday gatherings. The marinade used in this recipe adds a sweet and tangy flavor to the herring slices, which pairs well with the red onion, cucumber, and fresh dill. Proper food safety practices, such as using clean and sterilized jars, should be followed when making preserved foods.

Ingredients (4 servings)
6 herring fillets, deboned and cut into thin slices
1 red onion, thinly sliced
1 cucumber, thinly sliced
Fresh dill, chopped
Lemon slices, for garnish (optional)

Marinade
½ cup white vinegar
½ cup water
¼ cup sugar
½ teaspoon salt
¼ teaspoon black pepper
4-5 whole allspice berries
4-5 whole cloves

Preparation

In a saucepan, mix the white vinegar, water, sugar, salt, black pepper, allspice berries, and cloves. Bring this mixture to a boil, then reduce the heat to low and simmer for about 5 minutes, stirring occasionally to dissolve the sugar and salt. Remove from heat and let the marinade cool completely. Once the marinade is cooled, place the herring slices, red onion slices, and cucumber slices in a clean, sterilized glass jar, layering them alternately.

Pour the cooled marinade over the herring slices in the jar, making sure that the slices are fully submerged in the marinade. Add chopped fresh dill on top of the herring slices in the jar. Close the jar with airtight lid and refrigerate for at least 24 hours, or preferably 2-3 days, to allow the flavors to meld and the herring to fully marinate. Serve the herring slices chilled, garnished with lemon slices, if desired. They can be enjoyed as a delicious and traditional Estonian appetizer or snack.

Estonian breadsticks (Leivasnäkid)

Preparation time: 15 minutes
Cook time: 20 minutes
Nutrition facts (per serving): 221 Cal (12g fat, 3.2g protein, 4g fiber)

Leivasnäkid, or Estonian breadsticks, are a popular snack in Estonia that are often served with soups, dips, or as a standalone snack. They're typically crispy and slightly salty, making them a delicious and satisfying treat. This recipe yields homemade breadsticks that are easy to make and perfect for snacking.

Ingredients (8 servings)
2 cups all-purpose flour
½ teaspoon salt
½ teaspoon sugar
1 teaspoon active dry yeast
2 tablespoons vegetable oil
½ cup lukewarm water
Sesame seeds or poppy seeds, for topping (optional)

Preparation
In a suitable mixing bowl, whisk the flour, salt, sugar, and yeast. Stir in the vegetable oil and lukewarm water to the dry ingredients, and mix until a dough forms. Knead this dough on a floured surface for about 5 minutes, until it becomes smooth and elastic. Place this dough back in

the mixing bowl, cover it with a clean cloth, and let it rise in a warm place for about 1 hour, until it has doubled in size.

At 350°F, preheat your oven and line a baking sheet with parchment paper. Punch down the risen dough, and transfer it to a floured surface. Divide this dough into small pieces, and roll each piece into a thin rope or stick shape. Place this dough ropes onto the prepared baking sheet, leaving some space between them. If desired, you can drizzle the breadsticks with sesame seeds or poppy seeds for added flavor and crunch. Bake the breadsticks in the preheated oven for about 15-20 minutes, until they are golden brown and crispy. Remove the breadsticks from the oven and let them cool on the baking sheet before serving.

Estonian pickles (Hapukurk)

Preparation time: 15 minutes
Nutrition facts (per serving): 212 Cal (16g fat, 5g protein, 4g fiber)

Hapukurk, or Estonian pickles, are a popular traditional snack in Estonia. They are typically made from pickling cucumbers, vinegar, and a mixture of spices, and are known for their tangy and slightly sweet flavor. This simple recipe allows you to make your own batch of delicious homemade pickles that can be enjoyed on their own or as a condiment with various dishes.

Ingredients (8 servings)
2 lbs. pickling cucumbers
3 cloves of garlic, peeled
3 dill sprigs
1 tablespoon whole black peppercorns
1 tablespoon salt
1 tablespoon sugar
4 cups water
1 cup vinegar (white or apple cider vinegar)

Preparation
Wash the pickling cucumbers thoroughly and remove any dirt or debris. Place the cucumbers in a clean glass jar or container, along with the peeled garlic cloves, dill sprigs, and black peppercorns. In a saucepan, mix the water, salt, sugar, and vinegar. Bring this mixture to a boil, and then

remove it from the heat. Carefully pour the hot vinegar mixture over the cucumbers in the jar, covering them completely.

Place a clean lid or plastic wrap over the jar, and leave it to cool to room temperature. Once the pickle brine has cooled, cover the jar tightly and refrigerate it for at least 24 hours before serving. The pickles will continue to develop flavor as they marinate in the brine, so the longer they sit, the more flavorful they will become. Enjoy the homemade Estonian pickles as a tangy and crunchy snack, or as a side dish with your favorite Estonian meal.

Kohuke

Preparation time: 20 minutes
Nutrition facts (per serving): 159 Cal (9g fat, 4g protein, 4g fiber)

Kohuke is a popular Estonian snack made from quark cheese, which is a type of fresh cheese commonly used in Estonian cuisine. These quark snacks are typically sweetened with honey and flavored with vanilla, and often rolled in crushed digestive or graham crackers for a crunchy coating. Shredded coconut or chopped nuts can also be added for additional texture and flavor. These kohukesed can be enjoyed as a wholesome and delicious snack for a taste of Estonian culinary tradition.

Ingredients (4 servings)
1 cup quark cheese
2 tablespoons honey
1 teaspoon vanilla extract
½ cup crushed digestive or graham crackers
¼ cup shredded coconut or chopped nuts (optional)

Preparation
In a suitable mixing bowl, mix the quark cheese, honey, and vanilla extract. Stir well to incorporate the ingredients. Stir in the crushed digestive or graham crackers to the quark mixture. Stir to combine. Taste this mixture and adjust the sweetness with additional honey if desired. If using shredded coconut or chopped nuts, mix them into the quark mixture. Using a spoon or your hands, shape the quark mixture into small balls or patties. Place the quark snacks on a plate or tray and refrigerate

for at least 1 hour to firm up. Once chilled, the Estonian quark snacks, or kohukesed, are ready to be served as a delightful and healthy snack.

Kama Kottidega

Preparation time: 15 minutes
Nutrition facts (per serving): 203 Cal (15g fat, 7g protein, 4g fiber)

This recipe is a simple and easy way to enjoy the flavors of Estonia with these delightful kama pouches that can be served as a snack or dessert for a taste of Estonian culinary tradition.

Ingredients (2 servings)
1 cup kama (roasted grain mixture)
1 cup plain yogurt
½ cup mixed berries (blueberries, raspberries, strawberries)
2 tablespoons honey
Fresh mint leaves, for garnish (optional)

Preparation
In a suitable mixing bowl, mix the kama and plain yogurt. Stir well to form a thick, smooth mixture. Wash the mixed berries and drain them. If using strawberries, hull and chop them into smaller pieces. Stir in the mixed berries and honey to the kama-yogurt mixture. Stir gently to combine. Taste this mixture and adjust the sweetness to your preference with additional honey, if needed. Using a spoon or your hands, form small pouches or balls with the kama mixture. You can shape them into small balls or flatten them into discs. Arrange the kama pouches on a serving plate. Garnish with fresh mint leaves, if desired, for an extra touch of freshness. Serve the kama pouches chilled as a healthy and refreshing Estonian snack or dessert.

Ham and Cheese Buns

Preparation time: 10 minutes
Cook time: 25 minutes
Nutrition facts (per serving): 232 Cal (14g fat, 10g protein, 1.3g fiber)

Saiake või singiga, or Estonian ham and cheese buns, are a popular snack or appetizer in Estonia. These savory buns are made with a yeasted dough that's filled with ham, cheese, and a creamy mayonnaise-mustard mixture for a flavorful and indulgent treat. They're perfect for parties, picnics, or as a tasty snack any time of the day. Enjoy these delicious Estonian ham and cheese buns as a delightful and satisfying snack!

Ingredients (8 servings)
Dough
2 cups all-purpose flour
1 teaspoon active dry yeast
1 teaspoon salt
2 tablespoons sugar
½ cup milk
½ cup water
¼ cup butter, melted
1 large egg

Filling
½ lb. ham slices
½ lb. cheese slices (such as Gouda or Swiss)
¼ cup mayonnaise
1 tablespoon Dijon mustard
1 tablespoon fresh parsley, chopped (optional)

Preparation

In a suitable mixing bowl, whisk the flour, yeast, salt, and sugar. In a saucepan, warm the milk and water until it reaches about 110°F (43°C). Stir in the warm milk mixture, melted butter, and egg to the dry ingredients. Stir until a dough forms. Turn this dough out onto a floured surface and knead for 5-7 minutes until smooth and elastic. Place this dough back in the mixing bowl and cover with a clean towel. Let it rise in a warm, draft-free place for 1 hour until doubled in size. Meanwhile, prepare the filling by combining the mayonnaise, Dijon mustard, and chopped parsley (if using) in a suitable bowl.

At 375°F, preheat your oven and grease a baking sheet. Once this dough has risen, punch it down and turn it out onto a floured surface. Roll out this dough into a suitable rectangle about ¼-inch thick. Spread the mayonnaise-mustard mixture evenly over this dough, leaving about ½-inch border around the edges. Layer the ham slices and cheese slices on top of the filling. Roll up this dough tightly, starting from the long side, into a log shape. Cut the log into 1-inch slices using a sharp knife or a piece of dental floss. Place the slices on the prepared baking sheet and brush the tops with melted butter. Bake in the preheated oven for 20-25 minutes, until the buns are golden brown and the cheese is melted and bubbly. Remove from the oven and let the buns cool slightly before serving.

Estonian Potato Balls (Kartulipallid)

Preparation time: 10 minutes
Cook time: 16 minutes
Nutrition facts (per serving): 252 Cal (6g fat, 9g protein, 7g fiber)

Kartulipallid, or Estonian Potato Balls, are a popular Estonian dish that can be enjoyed as a side dish, appetizer, or snack. Made with simple ingredients like potatoes, onions, and seasonings, these crispy and flavorful potato balls are easy to create and are sure to please your taste buds.

Ingredients (4 servings)
4 medium potatoes, peeled and boiled until tender
1 small onion, finely chopped
2 eggs
½ cup all-purpose flour
½ teaspoon salt
¼ teaspoon black pepper
Cooking oil, for frying

Preparation
In a suitable bowl, mash the boiled potatoes using a potato masher or fork until smooth. Stir in the chopped onion, eggs, flour, black pepper and salt to the mashed potatoes. Mix well to form a thick batter-like consistency. Heat enough cooking oil in a frying pan or deep fryer to cover the bottom of the pan or reach a depth of about ½ inch. Drop

spoonfuls of the potato mixture into the hot oil, forming small balls. Flatten slightly with the back of a spoon to form a round shape. Fry the potato balls on medium heat for about 3-4 minutes on each side, until golden brown and crispy. Remove the potato balls from the oil and place them on paper towels to drain any excess oil. Serve the Kartulipallid hot as a side dish, appetizer, or snack. They can be served with sour cream, ketchup, or any dipping sauce of your choice.

Estonian carrot slices (Porgandiviilud Hapukoorega)

Preparation time: 10 minutes
Cook time: 10 minutes
Nutrition facts (per serving): 142 Cal (5g fat, 6g protein, 1.2g fiber)

This snack is perfect for spring and summer gatherings or as a side dish for a light meal. Enjoy these refreshing and flavorful Estonian carrot slices with sour cream!

Ingredients (2 servings)
2 large carrots, peeled and sliced into thin rounds
½ cup sour cream
1 tablespoon fresh dill, chopped
1 tablespoon fresh parsley, chopped
Black pepper, to taste
Salt, to taste

Preparation
Fill a pot with water and bring it to a boil. Add a pinch of salt to the boiling water. Stir in the sliced carrots to the boiling water and cook for 2-3 minutes until they're just tender. Drain the carrots and rinse them with cold water to stop the cooking process. Let them cool completely. In a suitable bowl, mix the sour cream, chopped dill, chopped parsley, salt, and pepper. Stir well to combine. Place the cooled carrot slices on a serving platter. Drizzle the sour cream mixture over the carrot slices, covering them evenly. Garnish with additional chopped dill and parsley, if desired. Serve the Estonian carrot slices with sour cream as a refreshing and healthy snack or side dish.

Marinated Mushrooms

Preparation time: 10 minutes
Cook time: 15 minutes
Nutrition facts (per serving): 250 Cal (9.8g fat, 8g protein, 4g fiber)

These Estonian marinated mushrooms can be served as a side dish, appetizer, or as part of a charcuterie or antipasto platter. Enjoy the tangy and flavorful taste of these marinated mushrooms as a delicious Estonian snack or appetizer!

Ingredients (2 servings)
1 lb. fresh mushrooms, cleaned and halved
1 small onion, thinly sliced
2 cloves garlic, minced
½ cup white wine vinegar
½ cup water
¼ cup sugar, granulated
1 teaspoon salt
1 teaspoon whole black peppercorns
1 bay leaf
Fresh dill, for garnish

Preparation
In a suitable saucepan, mix the white wine vinegar, water, sugar, salt, whole black peppercorns, and bay leaf. Bring this mixture to a boil over medium heat, stirring to dissolve the sugar and salt. Stir in the sliced onion and minced garlic to the boiling liquid. Reduce the heat to low and simmer for 5 minutes, until the onion is slightly softened. Stir in the

cleaned and halved or quartered mushrooms to the saucepan. Stir gently to coat the mushrooms in the marinade. Simmer the mushrooms in the marinade for 10-15 minutes, until they're slightly softened but still firm to the bite. Remove the saucepan from the heat and let the marinated mushrooms cool to room temperature. Once cooled, transfer the marinated mushrooms and the marinade to a clean, airtight container. Cover and refrigerate for at least 24 hours to allow the flavors to meld and develop. When ready to serve, drain the marinated mushrooms from the marinade and transfer them to a serving dish. Garnish with fresh dill before serving.

Salads

Estonian Potato Salad

Preparation time: 15 minutes
Cook time: 15 minutes
Nutrition facts (per serving): 222 Cal (8g fat, 9g protein, 0.8g fiber)

Estonian Potato Salad is a classic and beloved dish in Estonian cuisine. It's typically made with boiled potatoes, boiled eggs, pickles, and a creamy dressing of mayonnaise or sour cream.

Ingredients (4 servings)
4 large potatoes, peeled and cubed
3 hard-boiled eggs, chopped
½ cup pickles, finely chopped
¼ cup red onion, finely chopped
½ cup mayonnaise
1 tablespoon Dijon mustard
1 tablespoon white vinegar
½ teaspoon salt
¼ teaspoon black pepper
Fresh dill or parsley, for garnish (optional)

Preparation
Place the cubed potatoes in a pot of salted water and bring to a boil. Cook until the potatoes are fork-tender, about 10-15 minutes. Drain and let them cool to room temperature. In a suitable mixing bowl, mix the boiled potatoes, chopped hard-boiled eggs, pickles, and red onion. In a suitable bowl, whisk the mayonnaise, Dijon mustard, white vinegar, black pepper and salt to make the dressing. Pour the dressing over the potato mixture

and gently toss until all the ingredients are well coated in the dressing. Taste and adjust seasoning as needed with black pepper and salt. Cover this bowl and refrigerate for at least 1 hour to allow the flavors to meld. When ready to serve, garnish with fresh dill or parsley, if desired. Serve chilled as a side dish or as part of a buffet spread for gatherings. Enjoy your homemade Estonian Potato Salad, a classic and delicious dish from Estonia!

Beet Salad (Punasepeedisalat)

Preparation time: 20 minutes
Nutrition facts (per serving): 221 Cal (12g fat, 3.2g protein, 4g fiber)

Beet Salad, also known as Punasepeedisalat in Estonian, is a popular side dish in Estonian cuisine. It's made with boiled beets, often combined with other vegetables and dressed with a tangy vinaigrette.

Ingredients (4 servings)
3 medium beets, boiled, peeled, and grated
1 small red onion, finely chopped
½ cup pickles, finely chopped
½ cup canned peas, drained
2 tablespoons white vinegar
2 tablespoons vegetable oil
1 teaspoon sugar
½ teaspoon salt
¼ teaspoon black pepper

Preparation
In a suitable mixing bowl, mix the grated boiled beets, chopped red onion, pickles, and canned peas. In a suitable bowl, whisk the white vinegar, vegetable oil, sugar, black pepper and salt to make the vinaigrette. Pour the vinaigrette over the beet mixture and toss gently until all the ingredients are well coated in the dressing. Taste and adjust seasoning as needed with salt, sugar, and black pepper. Cover this bowl and refrigerate

for at least 1 hour to allow the flavors to meld. When ready to serve, give the salad a final toss and transfer to a serving dish. Serve chilled as a side dish or as part of a buffet spread for gatherings. Enjoy your homemade Estonian Beet Salad, a delicious and colorful addition to your meal!

Mushroom Salad (Seenesalat)

Preparation time: 10 minutes
Nutrition facts (per serving): 171 Cal (3g fat, 2g protein, 4g fiber)

Mushroom Salad, also known as Seenesalat in Estonian, is a popular dish in Estonian cuisine, especially during the mushroom season in autumn. It's made with fresh or marinated mushrooms, often combined with other vegetables and dressed with a tangy vinaigrette.

Ingredients (2 servings)
1 lb. fresh mushrooms, cleaned and sliced or 1 lb. marinated mushrooms, drained
1 small red onion, finely chopped
½ cup pickles, finely chopped
½ cup canned peas, drained
2 tablespoons white vinegar
2 tablespoons vegetable oil
1 teaspoon sugar
½ teaspoon salt
¼ teaspoon black pepper

Preparation
If using fresh mushrooms, heat a pan over medium heat and add a little oil or butter. Stir in the sliced mushrooms and sauté until they release their moisture and turn golden brown. Remove from heat and let them cool to room temperature. If using marinated mushrooms, drain and skip

this step. In a suitable mixing bowl, mix the cooked mushrooms or marinated mushrooms, chopped red onion, pickles, and canned peas.

In a suitable bowl, whisk the white vinegar, vegetable oil, sugar, black pepper and salt to make the vinaigrette. Pour the vinaigrette over the mushroom mixture and toss gently until all the ingredients are well coated in the dressing. Taste and adjust the seasoning as needed with salt, sugar, and black pepper. Cover this bowl and refrigerate for at least 1 hour to allow the flavors to meld. When ready to serve, give the salad a final toss and transfer to a serving dish. Serve chilled as a side dish or as part of a buffet spread for gatherings. Enjoy your homemade Estonian Mushroom Salad, a delicious and earthy dish that celebrates the flavors of mushrooms!

Cucumber Salad (Kurgisalat)

Preparation time: 10 minutes
Nutrition facts (per serving): 71 Cal (3g fat, 2g protein, 4g fiber)

Cucumber Salad, also known as Kurgisalat in Estonian, is a refreshing and popular dish in Estonian cuisine. It's made with fresh cucumbers, often combined with onions and dressed with a tangy vinaigrette.

Ingredients (2 servings)
2 medium cucumbers, thinly sliced
1 small red onion, thinly sliced
2 tablespoons white vinegar
2 tablespoons vegetable oil
1 teaspoon sugar
½ teaspoon salt
¼ teaspoon black pepper
Fresh dill, for garnish (optional)

Preparation
In a suitable mixing bowl, mix the thinly sliced cucumbers and red onions. In a suitable bowl, whisk the white vinegar, vegetable oil, sugar, black pepper and salt to make the vinaigrette. Pour the vinaigrette over the cucumber and onion mixture and toss gently until all the ingredients are well coated in the dressing. Taste and adjust seasoning as needed with salt, sugar, and black pepper. Cover this bowl and refrigerate for at least 1 hour to allow the flavors to meld. When ready to serve, give the salad a

final toss and transfer to a serving dish. Garnish with fresh dill, if desired, for an extra burst of flavor. Serve chilled as a refreshing side dish or as part of a buffet spread for gatherings. Enjoy your homemade Estonian Cucumber Salad, a simple and delicious salad that is perfect for warm weather or as a light and refreshing side dish for any meal!

Herring Salad (Suitsusilli Salat)

Preparation time: 10 minutes
Nutrition facts (per serving): 221 Cal (12g fat, 3.2g protein, 4g fiber)

Herring Salad, also known as Suitsusilli salat in Estonian, is a traditional Estonian dish that features smoked herring as the main ingredient. It's typically served as a cold appetizer or side dish and is often enjoyed during festive occasions.

Ingredients (8 servings)
5 smoked herring fillets, skin removed
2 medium potatoes, boiled and diced
1 small red onion, finely chopped
1 small apple, peeled and diced
½ cup canned peas, drained
½ cup mayonnaise
2 tablespoons sour cream
1 tablespoon Dijon mustard
1 tablespoon fresh lemon juice
Black pepper, to taste
Salt, to taste
Fresh dill or chives, for garnish (optional)

Preparation
In a suitable mixing bowl, flake the smoked herring fillets into small pieces. Stir in the diced boiled potatoes, chopped red onion, diced apple,

and canned peas to the bowl with the herring. In a separate bowl, whisk the mayonnaise, sour cream, Dijon mustard, and lemon juice to make the dressing. Pour the dressing over the herring and vegetable mixture and toss gently until all the ingredients are well coated in the dressing. Taste and adjust seasoning as needed with black pepper and salt.

Cover this bowl and refrigerate for at least 1 hour to allow the flavors to meld. When ready to serve, give the salad a final toss and transfer to a serving dish. Garnish with fresh dill or chives, if desired, for added freshness and presentation. Serve chilled as a delicious and unique appetizer or side dish for festive occasions. Enjoy your homemade Estonian Herring Salad, a flavorful and satisfying dish that showcases the unique taste of smoked herring!

Carrot Salad (Porgandisalat)

Preparation time: 10 minutes
Nutrition facts (per serving): 211 Cal (6g fat, 5g protein, 4g fiber)

Carrot Salad, also known as Porgandisalat in Estonian, is a popular side dish in Estonian cuisine. It's made with fresh carrots and often combined with other vegetables and dressed with a simple vinaigrette.

Ingredients (4 servings)
4 medium carrots, peeled and grated
1 small red onion, finely chopped
1 small apple, peeled and grated
½ cup canned peas, drained
2 tablespoons white vinegar
2 tablespoons vegetable oil
1 teaspoon sugar
½ teaspoon salt
¼ teaspoon black pepper
Fresh parsley or dill, for garnish (optional)

Preparation
In a suitable mixing bowl, mix the grated carrots, chopped red onion, grated apple, and canned peas. In a suitable bowl, whisk the white vinegar, vegetable oil, sugar, black pepper and salt to make the vinaigrette. Pour the vinaigrette over the carrot and vegetable mixture and toss gently until all the ingredients are well coated in the dressing. Taste and adjust

seasoning as needed with salt, sugar, and black pepper. Cover this bowl and refrigerate for at least 1 hour to allow the flavors to meld. When ready to serve, give the salad a final toss and transfer to a serving dish. Garnish with fresh parsley or dill, if desired, for an extra burst of flavor and freshness. Serve chilled as a refreshing side dish for any meal. Enjoy your homemade Estonian Carrot Salad, a colorful and tasty side dish that complements a wide range of main courses!

Cabbage Salad (Kapsasalat)

Preparation time: 10 minutes
Nutrition facts (per serving): 182 Cal (1g fat, 0g protein, 1.3g fiber)

Cabbage Salad, also known as Kapsasalat in Estonian, is a popular salad in Estonian cuisine that features fresh cabbage as the main ingredient. It's typically dressed with a simple vinaigrette and often combined with other vegetables for added crunch and flavor.

Ingredients (4 servings)
4 cups green cabbage, finely shredded
1 small red onion, finely chopped
1 small carrot, peeled and grated
1 small apple, peeled and grated
2 tablespoons white vinegar
2 tablespoons vegetable oil
1 teaspoon sugar
½ teaspoon salt
¼ teaspoon black pepper
Fresh parsley or dill, for garnish (optional)

Preparation
In a suitable mixing bowl, mix the shredded cabbage, chopped red onion, grated carrot, and grated apple. In a suitable bowl, whisk the white vinegar, vegetable oil, sugar, black pepper and salt to make the vinaigrette. Pour the vinaigrette over the cabbage and vegetable mixture and toss

gently until all the ingredients are well coated in the dressing. Taste and adjust seasoning as needed with salt, sugar, and black pepper.

Cover this bowl and refrigerate for at least 1 hour to allow the flavors to meld. When ready to serve, give the salad a final toss and transfer to a serving dish. Garnish with fresh parsley or dill, if desired, for added freshness and presentation. Serve chilled as a crunchy and refreshing side dish for any meal. Enjoy your homemade Estonian Cabbage Salad, a simple and delicious salad that complements a wide range of main courses and adds a healthy dose of vegetables to your meal!

Tomato And Cucumber Salad (Tomati-Kurgisalat)

Preparation time: 10 minutes
Nutrition facts (per serving): 152 Cal (6g fat, 9g protein, 7g fiber)

Tomato and Cucumber Salad, also known as Tomati-kurgisalat in Estonian, is a refreshing and simple salad that features fresh tomatoes and cucumbers as the main ingredients. It's often served as a side dish in Estonian cuisine and is perfect for warm weather when fresh produce is abundant.

Ingredients (4 servings)
2 large tomatoes, diced
1 large cucumber, peeled and diced
1 small red onion, finely chopped
2 tablespoons white vinegar
2 tablespoons vegetable oil
1 teaspoon sugar
½ teaspoon salt
¼ teaspoon black pepper
Fresh parsley or dill, for garnish (optional)

Preparation
In a suitable mixing bowl, mix the diced tomatoes, diced cucumber, and chopped red onion. In a suitable bowl, whisk the white vinegar, vegetable oil, sugar, black pepper and salt to make the vinaigrette. Pour the vinaigrette over the tomato and cucumber mixture and toss gently until

all the ingredients are well coated in the dressing. Taste and adjust the seasoning as needed with salt, sugar, and black pepper.

Cover this bowl and refrigerate for at least 30 minutes to allow the flavors to meld and the salad to chill. When ready to serve, give the salad a final toss and transfer to a serving dish. Garnish with fresh parsley or dill, if desired, for added freshness and presentation. Serve chilled as a light and refreshing side dish for any meal. Enjoy your homemade Estonian Tomato and Cucumber Salad, a perfect salad for showcasing the flavors of fresh tomatoes and cucumbers in a simple yet delicious way!

Mixed Salad (Segasalat)

Preparation time: 10 minutes
Nutrition facts (per serving): 232 Cal (1g fat, 7g protein, 1.3g fiber)

Mixed Salad, also known as Segasalat in Estonian, is a versatile salad that combines various vegetables, often including potatoes, beets, carrots, and peas, in a tangy vinaigrette dressing. It's a popular salad in Estonian cuisine and can be served as a side dish or a main course.

Ingredients (4 servings)
2 medium potatoes, peeled and boiled until fork-tender
2 medium beets, peeled, boiled until fork-tender, and diced
2 medium carrots, peeled, boiled until fork-tender, and diced
1 cup frozen peas, thawed
1 small red onion, finely chopped
2 tablespoons white vinegar
2 tablespoons vegetable oil
1 teaspoon sugar
½ teaspoon salt
¼ teaspoon black pepper
Fresh parsley or dill, for garnish (optional)

Preparation
In a suitable mixing bowl, mix the diced boiled potatoes, diced boiled beets, diced boiled carrots, thawed peas, and chopped red onion. In a suitable bowl, whisk the white vinegar, vegetable oil, sugar, black pepper

and salt to make the vinaigrette. Pour the vinaigrette over the mixed vegetables and toss gently until all the ingredients are well coated in the dressing. Taste and adjust seasoning as needed with salt, sugar, and black pepper.

Cover this bowl and refrigerate for at least 1 hour to allow the flavors to meld and the salad to chill. When ready to serve, give the salad a final toss and transfer to a serving dish. Garnish with fresh parsley or dill, if desired, for added freshness and presentation. Serve chilled as a delicious and colorful side dish or a light and healthy main course.

Soups

Pea Soup
(Hernesupp)

Preparation time: 10 minutes
Cook time: 60 minutes
Nutrition facts (per serving): 257 Cal (14g fat, 19g protein, 3.4g fiber)

Hernesupp, Estonian pea soup, is a comforting and hearty dish made with dried yellow peas, vegetables, and often smoked pork, offering a flavorful and satisfying bowl of warmth that's a beloved staple in Estonian cuisine.

Ingredients (4 servings)
1 cup dried yellow peas
1 large onion, chopped
2 carrots, peeled and diced
2 potatoes, peeled and diced
8 oz. smoked pork or bacon, cubed
1 bay leaf
1 teaspoon thyme, dried
Black pepper, to taste
Salt, to taste
Fresh dill, for garnish (optional)

Preparation
Rinse the dried peas in cold water and soak them in water overnight or for at least 6 hours. Drain the soaked peas and transfer them to a suitable soup pot. Add enough water to cover the peas by about 2 inches. Stir in

the chopped onion, diced carrots, diced potatoes, smoked pork or bacon, bay leaf, and dried thyme to the pot. Bring the soup to a boil over medium-high heat, then reduce the heat to low and let it simmer for about 1 hour, until the peas and vegetables are tender. Liberally season the soup with black pepper and salt to taste. Remove the bay leaf and discard. Serve hot, garnished with fresh dill if desired. Enjoy your traditional Estonian Pea Soup (Hernesupp)!

Estonian Pumpkin Puree Soup (Kõrvitsapüreesupp)

Preparation time: 10 minutes
Cook time: 29 minutes
Nutrition facts (per serving): 519 Cal (24g fat, 24g protein, 14g fiber)

Kõrvitsapüreesupp, Estonian pumpkin puree soup, is a creamy and aromatic dish made with locally grown pumpkins, onions, and warming spices, offering a delicious and comforting soup that's enjoyed during the autumn season in Estonian cuisine.

Ingredients (4 servings)
1 small pumpkin (about 2 lbs.), peeled, seeded, and chopped into small cubes
1 large onion, chopped
2 cloves garlic, minced
2 medium carrots, peeled and chopped
2 medium potatoes, peeled and chopped
4 cups vegetable broth
1 cup heavy cream
2 tablespoons butter
1 teaspoon thyme, dried
Black pepper, to taste
Salt, to taste
Fresh parsley, for garnish (optional)

Preparation

In a suitable pot, melt the butter over medium heat. Stir in the chopped onion and minced garlic and sauté for 3-4 minutes, until softened. Stir in the chopped pumpkin, carrots, potatoes, and dried thyme to the pot. Stir to combine. Pour in the vegetable broth and bring to a boil. Reduce the heat to low, cover the pot, and simmer for 20-25 minutes, until the vegetables are tender. Remove the pot from the heat and let the soup cool slightly.

Use an immersion blender or a regular blender to puree the soup until smooth. Return the soup to the pot, stir in the heavy cream, and stir to combine. Heat the soup over low heat until warmed through, but do not boil. Liberally season the soup with black pepper and salt to taste. Ladle the hot pumpkin puree soup into bowls and garnish with fresh parsley, if desired. Serve hot and enjoy your delicious Estonian Pumpkin Puree Soup!

Mushroom Soup (Seenesupp)

Preparation time: 10 minutes
Cook time: 32 minutes
Nutrition facts (per serving): 332 Cal (14g fat, 10g protein, 1.3g fiber)

Seenesupp, Estonian mushroom soup, is a rich and earthy dish made with locally foraged mushrooms, often combined with potatoes, cream, and aromatic herbs, offering a flavorful and comforting bowl of goodness that celebrates Estonia's natural bounty.

Ingredients (4 servings)
1 lb. fresh mushrooms, sliced
1 large onion, chopped
2 cloves garlic, minced
3 tablespoons butter
3 tablespoons all-purpose flour
4 cups vegetable or mushroom broth
1 bay leaf
1 teaspoon thyme, dried
1 cup heavy cream
Black pepper, to taste
Salt, to taste
Fresh parsley, for garnish (optional)

Preparation

In a suitable soup pot, melt the butter over medium heat. Stir in the chopped onion and minced garlic, and sauté for 5-7 minutes, until the onion is soft and translucent. Stir in the sliced mushrooms to the pot and sauté for another 5-7 minutes, until the mushrooms release their liquid and start to brown. Drizzle the flour over the mushrooms and stir well to combine. Cook for 2-3 minutes, stirring constantly, to make a roux.

Gradually pour in the vegetable or mushroom broth, stirring constantly to avoid lumps. Stir in the bay leaf and dried thyme to the pot. Bring the soup to a boil, then reduce the heat to low and let it simmer for about 15 minutes, until the mushrooms are tender and the flavors have melded together. Remove the bay leaf and discard. Stir in the heavy cream and cook for another 5 minutes, stirring occasionally. Liberally season the soup with black pepper and salt to taste.

Remove the pot from the heat and let the soup cool slightly. Use an immersion blender or a regular blender to puree the soup until smooth, if desired. Reheat the soup over low heat, if needed before serving. Garnish with fresh parsley, if desired, and enjoy your delicious Estonian Mushroom Soup (Seenesupp)!

Estonian Pea Soup (Kaalika-Hernesupp)

Preparation time: 15 minutes
Cook time: 46 minutes
Nutrition facts (per serving): 236 Cal (13.8g fat, 18g protein, 1.7g fiber)

Kaalika-Hernesupp is a traditional Estonian soup that's often enjoyed during the colder months. It's a hearty and flavorful soup that showcases the natural sweetness of rutabaga and peas. It can be served as a starter or a main dish, and it's often accompanied by Estonian rye bread or other breads for a complete meal.

Ingredients (4 servings)
1 tablespoon vegetable oil
1 onion, finely chopped
2 cloves garlic, minced
1 rutabaga (about 1 lb.), peeled and diced
1 cup frozen peas
6 cups vegetable broth
2 bay leaves
1 teaspoon thyme, dried
½ teaspoon marjoram, dried
Black pepper, to taste
Salt, to taste
Fresh parsley, for garnish
Sour cream or yogurt, for serving (optional)

Preparation

Heat the vegetable oil in a suitable pot over medium heat. Stir in the chopped onion and minced garlic, and sauté for 2-3 minutes until softened. Stir in the diced rutabaga and frozen peas to the pot, and cook for another 2-3 minutes. Pour in the vegetable broth, and stir in the bay leaves, dried thyme, and dried marjoram. Season with black pepper and salt to taste. Bring the soup to a boil, then reduce the heat to low and let it simmer for about 30-40 minutes, until the rutabaga is tender. Remove the bay leaves and discard. Taste and adjust the seasoning as needed. Serve the Estonian Kaalika-Hernesupp hot, garnished with fresh parsley. Optionally, you can serve the soup with a dollop of sour cream or yogurt on top for added creaminess. Enjoy your delicious Estonian Rutabaga and Pea Soup!

Fish Soup
(Kalasupp)

Preparation time: 10 minutes
Cook time: 30 minutes
Nutrition facts (per serving): 432 Cal (10g fat, 22g protein, 1.3g fiber)

Kalasupp, Estonian fish soup, is a flavorful and hearty dish made with fresh fish, vegetables, and often potatoes, simmered in a savory broth with herbs and spices, offering a taste of the Baltic Sea's bounty and a beloved delicacy in Estonian cuisine.

Ingredients (4 servings)
1 lb. white fish fillets, such as cod or haddock, cut into bite-sized pieces
1 large onion, chopped
2 carrots, peeled and diced
2 potatoes, peeled and diced
1 leek, cleaned and sliced
2 tablespoons butter
4 cups fish or vegetable broth
1 bay leaf
1 teaspoon thyme, dried
1 cup heavy cream
Black pepper, to taste
Salt, to taste
Fresh dill, for garnish (optional)

Preparation

In a suitable soup pot, melt the butter over medium heat. Stir in the chopped onion, diced carrots, diced potatoes, and sliced leek, and sauté for 5-7 minutes, until the vegetables are softened. Stir in the fish fillets to the pot and sauté for another 2-3 minutes, until they're partially cooked. Pour in the fish or vegetable broth, and stir in the bay leaf and dried thyme to the pot. Bring the soup to a boil, then reduce the heat to low and let it simmer for about 15 minutes, until the fish and vegetables are fully cooked and tender.

Remove the bay leaf and discard. Stir in the heavy cream and cook for another 5 minutes, stirring occasionally. Liberally season the soup with black pepper and salt to taste. Remove the pot from the heat and let the soup cool slightly. Use an immersion blender or a regular blender to puree the soup until smooth, if desired. Reheat the soup over low heat if needed before serving. Garnish with fresh dill if desired, and enjoy your tasty Estonian Fish Soup (Kalasupp)!

Beet Soup (Borsisupp)

Preparation time: 10 minutes
Cook time: 41 minutes
Nutrition facts (per serving): 112 Cal (5g fat, 5g protein, 2g fiber)

Borsisupp, Estonian beet soup, is a vibrant and tangy dish made with beets, cabbage, and often meat, simmered in a sour and slightly sweet broth, offering a unique and delicious flavor profile that's a cherished part of Estonian culinary heritage.

Ingredients (4 servings)
2 medium beets, peeled and grated
1 medium onion, chopped
2 carrots, peeled and grated
2 potatoes, peeled and diced
1 tablespoon butter
4 cups beef or vegetable broth
2 bay leaves
1 teaspoon thyme, dried
2 tablespoons tomato paste
2 tablespoons red wine vinegar
2 tablespoons sugar
Black pepper, to taste
Salt, to taste
Sour cream, for serving
Fresh dill, for garnish (optional)

Preparation

In a suitable soup pot, melt the butter over medium heat. Stir in the chopped onion and sauté for 3-4 minutes, until softened. Stir in the grated beets, grated carrots, and diced potatoes to the pot, and sauté for another 3-4 minutes. Pour in the beef or vegetable broth, and stir in the bay leaves, dried thyme, tomato paste, red wine vinegar, and sugar to the pot. Bring the soup to a boil, then reduce the heat to low and let it simmer for about 30 minutes, until the vegetables are fully cooked and tender. Remove the bay leaves and discard. Liberally season the soup with black pepper and salt to taste. Remove the pot from the heat and let the soup cool slightly. Use an immersion blender or a regular blender to puree the soup until smooth, if desired. Reheat the soup over low heat if needed before serving. Serve the beet soup hot, garnished with a dollop of sour cream and fresh dill, if desired. Enjoy your delicious Estonian Beet Soup (Boršisupp) with its vibrant color and rich flavors!

Sauerkraut Soup (Hapukapsasupp)

Preparation time: 15 minutes
Cook time: 48 minutes
Nutrition facts (per serving): 688 Cal (35.9g fat, 36.9g protein, 2.1g fiber)

Hapukapsasupp, Estonian sauerkraut soup, is a tangy and hearty dish made with fermented cabbage, often combined with pork, potatoes, and warming spices, offering a flavorful and comforting bowl of soup that is a beloved winter staple in Estonian cuisine.

Ingredients (4 servings)
2 cups sauerkraut, rinsed and drained
1 large onion, finely chopped
2 medium carrots, peeled and grated
2 medium potatoes, peeled and diced
2 tablespoons vegetable oil
1 tablespoon tomato paste
1 bay leaf
1 teaspoon caraway seeds
1 teaspoon thyme, dried
4 cups vegetable or beef broth
2 cups water
Black pepper, to taste
Salt, to taste
Sour cream, for serving
Fresh parsley, for garnish (optional)

Preparation

Heat the vegetable oil in a suitable soup pot over medium heat. Stir in the chopped onion and sauté for 3-4 minutes, until softened. Stir in the grated carrots and diced potatoes to the pot, and sauté for another 3-4 minutes. Stir in the sauerkraut, tomato paste, bay leaf, caraway seeds, and dried thyme. Cook for another 2-3 minutes, stirring occasionally. Pour in the vegetable or beef broth, and stir in the water to the pot. Bring the soup to a boil, then reduce the heat to low and let it simmer for about 30-40 minutes, until the vegetables are fully cooked and tender.

Remove the bay leaf and discard. Liberally season the soup with black pepper and salt to taste. Remove the pot from the heat and let the soup cool slightly. Reheat the soup over low heat, if needed before serving. Serve the sauerkraut soup hot, garnished with a dollop of sour cream and fresh parsley, if desired. Enjoy your delicious Estonian Sauerkraut Soup (Hapukapsasupp) with its tangy and hearty flavors!

Barley Soup (Odrasupp)

Preparation time: 15 minutes
Cook time: 81 minutes
Nutrition facts (per serving): 367 Cal (7.7g fat, 4.5g protein, 1g fiber)

Odrasupp, Estonian barley soup, is a nourishing and wholesome dish made with pearl barley, vegetables, and often meat, simmered to perfection in a flavorful broth, offering a hearty and satisfying bowl of soup that's a cherished part of Estonian culinary tradition.

Ingredients (4 servings)

1 cup pearl barley
1 large onion, finely chopped
2 medium carrots, peeled and diced
2 medium potatoes, peeled and diced
2 tablespoons vegetable oil
1 bay leaf
1 teaspoon thyme, dried
4 cups vegetable or beef broth
4 cups water
Black pepper, to taste
Salt, to taste
Fresh parsley, for garnish (optional)

Preparation

Rinse the pearl barley under cold water and drain. Heat the vegetable oil in a suitable soup pot over medium heat. Stir in the chopped onion and sauté for 3-4 minutes, until softened. Stir in the diced carrots and potatoes to the pot, and sauté for another 3-4 minutes. Stir in the pearl barley, bay leaf, and dried thyme. Cook for another 2-3 minutes, stirring occasionally. Pour in the vegetable or beef broth, and stir in the water to the pot. Bring the soup to a boil, then reduce the heat to low and let it simmer for about 45-60 minutes, until the barley and vegetables are fully cooked and tender. Remove the bay leaf and discard. Liberally season the soup with black pepper and salt to taste. Remove the pot from the heat and let the soup cool slightly. Reheat the soup over low heat, if needed before serving. Serve the barley soup hot, garnished with fresh parsley, if desired. Enjoy your delicious Estonian Barley Soup (Odrasupp) with its hearty and wholesome flavors!

Cabbage Soup

Preparation time: 10 minutes
Cook time: 35 minutes
Nutrition facts (per serving): 234 Cal (7.7g fat, 8.8g protein, 4g fiber)

Kapsasupp, Estonian cabbage soup, is a hearty and flavorful dish made with cabbage, potatoes, and often meat, simmered together in a tangy and aromatic broth for a comforting and nourishing meal that's a staple in Estonian culinary tradition.

Ingredients (4 servings)
1 small head of cabbage, shredded
1 large onion, finely chopped
2 carrots, peeled and grated
2 potatoes, peeled and diced
1 tablespoon vegetable oil
4 cups vegetable broth
1 bay leaf
1 teaspoon thyme, dried
Black pepper, to taste
Salt, to taste
Fresh parsley, for garnish
Sour cream, for serving (optional)

Preparation
Heat the vegetable oil in a suitable pot over medium heat. Stir in the chopped onion and grated carrots to the pot and sauté for 5 minutes, until the vegetables are softened. Stir in the shredded cabbage to the pot

and cook for another 5 minutes, stirring occasionally. Stir in the diced potatoes, vegetable broth, bay leaf, dried thyme, salt, and pepper to the pot. Bring this mixture to a boil. Reduce the heat to low and let the soup simmer for about 20-25 minutes, until the vegetables are tender. Remove the bay leaf from the soup and discard. Taste the soup and adjust seasoning with black pepper and salt, if needed. Serve hot, garnished with fresh parsley.

Estonian sauerkraut soup (Hapukapsasupp)

Preparation time: 20 minutes
Cook time: 25 minutes
Nutrition facts (per serving): 264 Cal (6.1g fat, 10.3 protein, 4g fiber)

Hapukapsasupp, Estonian sauerkraut soup, is a tangy and hearty dish made with fermented cabbage, often combined with pork, potatoes, and warming spices, offering a flavorful and comforting bowl of soup that's a beloved winter staple in Estonian cuisine.

Ingredients (4 servings)

1 cup sauerkraut
1 large onion, finely chopped
2 carrots, peeled and grated
2 potatoes, peeled and diced
1 tablespoon vegetable oil
4 cups vegetable or meat broth
1 bay leaf
1 teaspoon thyme, dried
Black pepper, to taste
Salt, to taste
Fresh parsley, for garnish
Sour cream, for serving (optional)

Preparation

Rinse the sauerkraut under cold water to remove excess brine and drain. Heat the vegetable oil in a suitable pot over medium heat. Stir in the chopped onion and grated carrots to the pot and sauté for 5 minutes, until the vegetables are softened. Stir in the sauerkraut, diced potatoes, vegetable or meat broth, bay leaf, dried thyme, salt, and pepper to the pot. Bring this mixture to a boil. Reduce the heat to low and let the soup simmer for about 20-25 minutes, until the vegetables are tender. Remove the bay leaf from the soup and discard. Taste the soup and adjust seasoning with black pepper and salt, if needed. Serve hot, garnished with fresh parsley. Optionally, you can serve with a dollop of sour cream on top. Enjoy your flavorful Estonian Sauerkraut Soup!

Main Dishes

Pork and Sauerkraut Stew (Seakapsahautis)

Preparation time: 15 minutes
Cook time: 70 minutes
Nutrition facts (per serving): 473 Cal (11g fat, 36g protein, 2g fiber)

Seakapsahautis, Estonian pork and sauerkraut stew, is a flavorful and hearty dish made with tender pork, tangy sauerkraut, and aromatic spices, slow-cooked to meld the flavors together, offering a deliciously comforting and satisfying meal that is a beloved part of Estonian cuisine.

Ingredients (4 servings)
1 lb. pork shoulder, cubed
1 onion, finely chopped
2 cloves garlic, minced
2 cups sauerkraut, drained
2 potatoes, peeled and cubed
2 carrots, peeled and diced
2 bay leaves
1 teaspoon caraway seeds
1 teaspoon salt
½ teaspoon black pepper
2 cups beef or vegetable broth
1 tablespoon vegetable oil
1 tablespoon butter
Fresh parsley, for garnish

Preparation

Heat the vegetable oil and butter in a suitable pot or Dutch oven over medium heat. Stir in the diced pork and cook until browned on all sides. Remove the pork from the pot and set aside. In the same pot, stir in the chopped onion and minced garlic. Cook until the onion is softened and translucent. Stir in the sauerkraut, potatoes, carrots, bay leaves, caraway seeds, black pepper and salt to the pot. Stir well to combine. Stir in the browned pork back to the pot, along with the beef or vegetable broth. Bring to a boil.

Reduce the heat to low, cover the pot, and simmer for about 1 hour until the pork is tender and the vegetables are cooked through. Taste and adjust seasoning with more black pepper and salt, if needed. Remove the bay leaves and discard. Serve hot, garnished with fresh parsley. Enjoy your delicious Estonian Pork and Sauerkraut Stew! It's a comforting and flavorful dish that is perfect for cold weather or whenever you crave a hearty meal.

Beef Stew (Hakklihahautis)

Preparation time: 15 minutes
Cook time: 40 minutes
Nutrition facts (per serving): 403 Cal (23g fat, 17g protein, 2g fiber)

Hakklihahautis, Estonian beef stew, is a rich and savory dish made with tender beef, vegetables, and aromatic herbs, slow-cooked to perfection for a flavorful and comforting meal that's a beloved classic in Estonian cuisine.

Ingredients (4 servings)
1 lb. ground beef
1 onion, finely chopped
2 cloves garlic, minced
2 carrots, peeled and diced
2 potatoes, peeled and cubed
2 bay leaves
1 teaspoon thyme, dried
1 teaspoon paprika
1 teaspoon salt
½ teaspoon black pepper
2 cups beef broth
1 tablespoon vegetable oil
1 tablespoon butter
Fresh parsley, for garnish

Preparation

Heat the vegetable oil and butter in a suitable pot or Dutch oven over medium heat. Stir in the chopped onion and minced garlic. Cook until the onion is softened and translucent. Stir in the ground beef to the pot and cook, breaking it up with a spoon, until browned. Stir in the diced carrots, cubed potatoes, bay leaves, dried thyme, paprika, black pepper and salt to the pot. Stir well to combine. Stir in the beef broth to the pot and bring to a boil. Reduce the heat to low, cover the pot, and simmer for about 30-40 minutes until the vegetables are tender. Taste and adjust seasoning with more black pepper and salt, if needed. Remove the bay leaves and discard. Serve hot, garnished with fresh parsley. Enjoy your delicious Estonian Beef Stew! It's a comforting and flavorful dish that is perfect for a hearty meal. Serve it with bread or mashed potatoes for a complete meal.

Chicken and Vegetable Stew (Kana- Ja Köögiviljahautis)

Preparation time: 15 minutes
Cook time: 40 minutes
Nutrition facts (per serving): 467 Cal (29g fat, 28g protein, 3g fiber)

Kana- ja köögiviljahautis, Estonian chicken and vegetable stew, is a wholesome and flavorful dish made with tender chicken, a medley of vegetables, and aromatic spices, simmered together to create a comforting and nourishing meal that's enjoyed in Estonian households.

Ingredients (2 servings)
1 lb. boneless, skinless chicken breasts or thighs, diced
1 onion, finely chopped
2 carrots, peeled and diced
2 potatoes, peeled and cubed
1 parsnip, peeled and diced
2 celery stalks, diced
2 bay leaves
1 teaspoon thyme, dried
1 teaspoon paprika
1 teaspoon salt
½ teaspoon black pepper
2 cups chicken broth
1 tablespoon vegetable oil
1 tablespoon butter
Fresh parsley, for garnish

Preparation

Heat the vegetable oil and butter in a suitable pot or Dutch oven over medium heat. Stir in the chopped onion to the pot and cook until softened and translucent. Stir in the diced chicken to the pot and cook until browned on all sides. Stir in the diced carrots, cubed potatoes, diced parsnip, diced celery, bay leaves, dried thyme, paprika, black pepper and salt to the pot. Stir well to combine. Stir in the chicken broth to the pot and bring to a boil.

Reduce the heat to low, cover the pot, and simmer for about 30-40 minutes until the vegetables are tender and the chicken is cooked through. Taste and adjust seasoning with more black pepper and salt, if needed. Remove the bay leaves and discard. Serve hot, garnished with fresh parsley. Enjoy your delicious Estonian Chicken and Vegetable Stew! It's a comforting and nutritious dish that's perfect for a hearty meal. Serve it with bread or rice for a complete meal.

Mushroom and Potato Stew (Seene- Ja Kartulihautis)

Preparation time: 15 minutes
Cook time: 30 minutes
Nutrition facts (per serving): 398 Cal (16g fat, 39g protein, 1.2g fiber)

Seene- ja kartulihautis, Estonian mushroom and potato stew, is a hearty and earthy dish made with locally foraged mushrooms, tender potatoes, and aromatic herbs, simmered to perfection for a flavorful and satisfying meal that's a beloved part of Estonian cuisine.

Ingredients (2 servings)
1 lb. fresh mushrooms, sliced
2 potatoes, peeled and cubed
1 onion, finely chopped
2 cloves garlic, minced
2 tablespoons butter
2 tablespoons all-purpose flour
2 cups vegetable broth
1 cup heavy cream
1 teaspoon thyme, dried
1 teaspoon salt
½ teaspoon black pepper
Fresh parsley, for garnish

Preparation

Heat the butter in a suitable pot or Dutch oven over medium heat. Stir in the chopped onion and minced garlic to the pot and cook until softened and fragrant. Stir in the sliced mushrooms to the pot and cook until they release their moisture and start to brown. Drizzle the flour over the mushrooms and stir well to coat. Stir in the cubed potatoes, vegetable broth, dried thyme, black pepper and salt to the pot. Stir well to combine. Bring this mixture to a boil, then reduce the heat to low, cover the pot, and simmer for about 15-20 minutes until the potatoes are tender.

Stir in the heavy cream and simmer for another 5 minutes. Taste and adjust seasoning with more black pepper and salt, if needed. Serve hot, garnished with fresh parsley. Enjoy your delicious Estonian Mushroom and Potato Stew! It's a creamy and flavorful dish that makes a satisfying meal. Serve it with bread or as a side dish for a complete meal.

Lamb Stew
(Lamba- Või Tallehautis)

Preparation time: 10 minutes
Cook time: 2 hours
Nutrition facts (per serving): 408 Cal (6.2g fat, 34g protein, 4g fiber)

Lamba- või tallehautis, Estonian lamb stew, is a succulent and flavorful dish made with tender lamb meat, vegetables, and aromatic spices, slow-cooked to perfection for a hearty and delicious meal that's a cherished part of Estonian culinary tradition.

Ingredients (4 servings)
2 lbs. lamb meat, cut into chunks
2 tablespoons vegetable oil
1 onion, finely chopped
2 carrots, peeled and diced
2 potatoes, peeled and diced
2 cloves garlic, minced
2 bay leaves
1 teaspoon thyme, dried
1 teaspoon salt
½ teaspoon black pepper
4 cups beef or lamb broth
1 cup red wine (optional)
Fresh parsley, for garnish

Preparation

Heat the vegetable oil in a suitable pot or Dutch oven over medium heat. Stir in the lamb meat to the pot and cook until browned on all sides. Remove the lamb meat from the pot and set aside. In the same pot, stir in the chopped onion, diced carrots, and minced garlic. Cook until the vegetables are softened. Stir in the diced potatoes, bay leaves, dried thyme, black pepper and salt to the pot. Stir well to combine. Return the lamb meat to the pot and stir in the beef or lamb broth, and red wine (if using).

Bring this mixture to a boil, then reduce the heat to low, cover the pot, and simmer for about 1 ½ to 2 hours, until the lamb is tender. Taste and adjust seasoning with more black pepper and salt, if needed. Serve hot, garnished with fresh parsley. Enjoy your delicious Estonian Lamb Stew! It's a flavorful and comforting dish that's perfect for colder weather. Serve it with bread or mashed potatoes for a complete meal.

Estonian Fish Stew (Kalaroog)

Preparation time: 20 minutes
Cook time: 25 minutes
Nutrition facts (per serving): 421 Cal (16g fat, 29g protein, 0g fiber)

Kalaroog, Estonian fish stew, is a delightful and flavorful dish made with fresh fish, vegetables, and herbs, simmered together in a savory broth for a taste of the Baltic Sea's bounty and a beloved delicacy in Estonian cuisine.

Ingredients (4 servings)
1 lb. fish fillets (such as cod, haddock, or salmon), cut into bite-sized pieces
1 onion, finely chopped
2 carrots, peeled and diced
2 potatoes, peeled and diced
2 celery stalks, diced
2 cloves garlic, minced
2 bay leaves
1 teaspoon dried dill
1 teaspoon salt
½ teaspoon black pepper
4 cups fish or vegetable broth
1 cup heavy cream
Fresh dill, for garnish

Preparation

In a suitable pot or Dutch oven, heat some oil or butter over medium heat. Stir in the chopped onion, diced carrots, celery, and minced garlic to the pot. Cook until the vegetables are softened. Stir in the diced potatoes, bay leaves, dried dill, black pepper and salt to the pot. Stir well to combine. Stir in the fish fillets and fish or vegetable broth to the pot. Bring this mixture to a boil, then reduce the heat to low, cover the pot, and simmer for about 15-20 minutes, until the fish is cooked through and the vegetables are tender. Stir in the heavy cream and cook for another 5 minutes.

Taste and adjust seasoning with more black pepper and salt, if needed. Remove the bay leaves from the stew before serving. Serve hot, garnished with fresh dill. Enjoy your delicious Estonian Fish Stew! It's a creamy and flavorful dish that highlights the fresh flavors of fish and vegetables. Serve it with bread or crackers for a satisfying meal.

Bean Stew
(Oa- Või Hernesupp)

Preparation time: 20 minutes
Cook time: 1 hour 30 minutes
Nutrition facts (per serving): 271 Cal (19g fat, 9g protein, 3g fiber)

Oa- või hernesupp, Estonian bean stew, is a hearty and nourishing dish made with tender beans, vegetables, and often smoked pork, simmered in a flavorful broth for a comforting and satisfying meal that's enjoyed in Estonian households.

Ingredients (4 servings)
2 cups dried beans (white beans, kidney beans, or black-eyed beans), soaked overnight and drained
1 onion, finely chopped
2 carrots, peeled and diced
2 potatoes, peeled and diced
2 celery stalks, diced
2 cloves garlic, minced
2 bay leaves
1 teaspoon thyme, dried
1 teaspoon salt
½ teaspoon black pepper
4 cups vegetable broth
1 cup tomato puree
Fresh parsley, for garnish

Preparation

In a suitable pot or Dutch oven, heat some oil or butter over medium heat. Stir in the chopped onion, diced carrots, celery, and minced garlic to the pot. Cook until the vegetables are softened. Stir in the soaked and drained beans, diced potatoes, bay leaves, dried thyme, salt, black pepper, vegetable broth, and tomato puree to the pot. Stir well to combine. Bring this mixture to a boil, then reduce the heat to low, cover the pot, and simmer for about 1 to 1 ½ hours, until the beans are cooked through and tender. Remove the bay leaves from the stew before serving. Taste and adjust seasoning with more black pepper and salt, if needed. Serve hot, garnished with fresh parsley.

Estonian Mushroom Rice Casserole (Seeneriis)

Preparation time: 20 minutes
Cook time: 40 minutes
Nutrition facts (per serving): 384 Cal (4.7g fat, 20g protein, 1.7g fiber)

Seeneriis, Estonian mushroom rice casserole, is a savory and creamy dish made with rice, locally foraged mushrooms, and aromatic spices, baked to perfection for a comforting and delicious meal that's a beloved part of Estonian cuisine.

Ingredients (4 servings)
1 cup long-grain white rice
2 cups water
½ teaspoon salt
4 tablespoons butter
1 medium onion, finely chopped
8 ounces fresh mushrooms, sliced
½ teaspoon thyme, dried
½ teaspoon dried marjoram
½ teaspoon salt
¼ teaspoon black pepper
2 tablespoons all-purpose flour
2 cups milk
1 cup grated cheese (such as Gouda, Cheddar, or Swiss)
Fresh parsley, chopped (optional)

Preparation

At 350°F, preheat your oven. Grease a 9x13 inch baking dish and set aside. In a saucepan, mix the rice, water, and ½ teaspoon of salt. Bring to a boil over medium heat, then reduce the heat to low, cover the pan, and simmer for about 15 minutes until the rice is cooked and the water is absorbed. In a suitable skillet, melt the butter over medium heat. Stir in the chopped onion and cook for about 5 minutes until softened. Stir in the sliced mushrooms, dried thyme, dried marjoram, ½ teaspoon of black pepper and salt to the skillet.

Cook for another 5 minutes until the mushrooms are tender. Stir in the flour and cook for 1 minute, stirring constantly. Gradually whisk in the milk, stirring constantly to avoid lumps. Cook for 5 minutes until the sauce thickens. Stir in the cooked rice and half of the grated cheese. Mix well. Pour the rice and mushroom mixture into the prepared baking dish. Drizzle the remaining grated cheese on top. Bake in the preheated oven for 25-30 minutes until the casserole is bubbly and the cheese is melted and golden on top. Remove from the oven and leave it to cool for a few minutes before serving. Garnish with chopped fresh parsley, if desired. Serve hot and enjoy!

Estonian Cabbage and Rice Casserole (Kapsa-Riisivorm)

Preparation time: 10 minutes
Cook time: 60 minutes
Nutrition facts (per serving): 449 Cal (3.6g fat, 17g protein, 5.4g fiber)

This Estonian Cabbage and Rice Casserole (Kapsa-riisivorm) is a hearty and flavorful dish that combines the sweetness of cabbage with the creaminess of rice and cheese. It's a classic Estonian comfort food that's perfect for cold weather or as a side dish for a holiday meal.

Ingredients (4 servings)
1 small head of cabbage, shredded
1 cup long-grain white rice
2 cups water
½ teaspoon salt
4 tablespoons butter
1 medium onion, finely chopped
2 cloves garlic, minced
1 teaspoon caraway seeds
½ teaspoon black pepper
½ teaspoon paprika
¼ teaspoon nutmeg
½ teaspoon salt
2 tablespoons all-purpose flour
2 cups milk
1 cup grated cheese (such as Gouda, Cheddar, or Swiss)
Fresh parsley, chopped (optional)

Preparation

At 350°F, preheat your oven. Grease a 9x13 inch baking dish and set aside. In a suitable pot of boiling water, blanch the shredded cabbage for 5 minutes. Drain and set aside. In a saucepan, mix the rice, water, and ½ teaspoon of salt. Bring to a boil over medium heat, then reduce the heat to low, cover the pan, and simmer for about 15 minutes until the rice is cooked and the water is absorbed. In a suitable skillet, melt the butter over medium heat. Stir in the chopped onion and cook for about 5 minutes until softened.

Stir in the minced garlic, caraway seeds, black pepper, paprika, nutmeg, and ½ teaspoon of salt to the skillet. Cook for another 2-3 minutes. Stir in the flour and cook for 1 minute, stirring constantly. Gradually whisk in the milk, stirring constantly to avoid lumps. Cook for 5 minutes until the sauce thickens. Stir in the blanched cabbage and cooked rice. Mix well. Pour the cabbage and rice mixture into the prepared baking dish. Drizzle the grated cheese on top.

Bake in the preheated oven for 25-30 minutes until the casserole is bubbly and the cheese is melted and golden on top. Remove from the oven and leave it to cool for a few minutes before serving. Garnish with chopped fresh parsley, if desired. Serve hot and enjoy!

Estonian Rice and Vegetable Stir-Fry (Riis Ja Köögiviljad Wokis)

Preparation time: 10 minutes
Cook time: 12 minutes
Nutrition facts (per serving): 372 Cal (29g fat, 21g protein, 1.4g fiber)

This dish is a simple and delicious way to enjoy rice and vegetables with a touch of Estonian flavors. It's a quick and easy stir-fry recipe that can be customized with your favorite vegetables and seasonings.

Ingredients (4 servings)
2 cups cooked white rice
1 cup mixed vegetables (such as carrots, bell peppers, peas, corn, etc.), chopped
1 small onion, finely chopped
2 cloves garlic, minced
2 tablespoons vegetable oil
2 tablespoons soy sauce
1 tablespoon oyster sauce (optional)
½ teaspoon salt
¼ teaspoon black pepper
Fresh cilantro or parsley, chopped (optional)

Preparation
Heat the vegetable oil in a wok or large skillet over high heat. Stir in the chopped onion and minced garlic to the wok and stir-fry for 1-2 minutes until fragrant. Stir in the mixed vegetables to the wok and stir-fry for

another 2-3 minutes until slightly tender. Stir in the cooked rice to the wok and stir-fry for another 2-3 minutes, stirring constantly to prevent sticking. Stir in the soy sauce and oyster sauce (if using) to the wok and stir-fry for another minute, until the sauce is well distributed and the rice and vegetables are evenly coated. Season with black pepper and salt to taste. Adjust the seasoning according to your preference. Remove from the heat and transfer to a serving dish. Garnish with fresh cilantro or parsley, if desired. Serve hot and enjoy your Estonian Rice and Vegetable Stir-Fry!

Estonian Oven-Baked Potatoes (Ahjukartulid)

Preparation time: 15 minutes
Cook time: 30 minutes
Nutrition facts (per serving): 273 Cal (23g fat, 8g protein, 2g fiber)

Ahjukartulid, Estonian oven-baked potatoes, are crispy and flavorful potatoes cooked in the oven with butter and spices, offering a delicious and comforting side dish that's a popular favorite in Estonian cuisine.

Ingredients (4 servings)
5 large potatoes, peeled and cut into small cubes
1 large onion, finely chopped
2 cloves garlic, minced
3 tablespoons vegetable oil
1 teaspoon thyme, dried
1 teaspoon paprika
Black pepper, to taste
Salt, to taste
Fresh parsley, for garnish (optional)

Preparation
At 400°F, preheat your oven. In a suitable bowl, toss the potato cubes with the chopped onion, minced garlic, vegetable oil, dried thyme, paprika, salt, and pepper. Make sure the potatoes are evenly coated with the seasoning mixture. Transfer the seasoned potatoes to a baking dish or sheet lined with parchment paper, spreading them out in an even layer.

Bake the potatoes in the preheated oven for 25-30 minutes, until they are golden brown and crispy on the outside, and tender on the inside. Stir the potatoes occasionally during baking to ensure even cooking. Remove the potatoes from the oven and let them cool slightly. Garnish with fresh parsley, if desired, and serve hot as a delicious side dish or snack. Enjoy your tasty Estonian Oven-Baked Potatoes!

Veggie Mince Sauce

Preparation time: 10 minutes
Cook time: 29 minutes
Nutrition facts (per serving): 109 Cal (4g fat, 29.5g protein, 3g fiber)

Estonian Veggie Mince Sauce is a popular comfort food in Estonia and can be served as a main dish or used as a filling for pies, pastries, or stuffed vegetables. It's a flavorful and hearty dish that's suitable for vegetarians and vegans.

Ingredients (4 servings)
1 tablespoon vegetable oil
1 onion, finely chopped
2 cloves garlic, minced
1 carrot, peeled and grated
1 small zucchini, grated
1 cup textured vegetable protein (TVP) or veggie mince
2 cups vegetable broth
1 tablespoon tomato paste
1 teaspoon paprika
½ teaspoon thyme, dried
½ teaspoon oregano, dried
1 bay leaf
½ cup tomato puree
1 tablespoon soy sauce
Black pepper, to taste
Salt, to taste
Fresh parsley, for garnish

Preparation

Heat the vegetable oil in a suitable skillet or pot over medium heat. Stir in the chopped onion and minced garlic, and sauté for 2-3 minutes until softened. Stir in the grated carrot and zucchini, and cook for another 2-3 minutes until they start to soften. Stir in the textured vegetable protein (TVP) or veggie mince to the skillet, and cook for 2-3 minutes until lightly browned. Stir in the vegetable broth, tomato paste, paprika, dried thyme, dried oregano, bay leaf, tomato puree, and soy sauce. Season with black pepper and salt to taste. Bring this mixture to a simmer, then reduce the heat to low and let it simmer for 15-20 minutes, stirring occasionally. Remove the bay leaf and discard. Taste and adjust the seasoning as needed. Serve the Estonian Veggie Mince Sauce hot over mashed potatoes, rice, or pasta. Garnish with fresh parsley before serving. Enjoy your delicious Veggie Mince Sauce!

Kõrvitsakotletid

Preparation time: 10 minutes
Cook time: 12 minutes
Nutrition facts (per serving): 232 Cal (14g fat, 10g protein, 1.3g fiber)

Kõrvitsakotletid are a popular Estonian dish made with grated pumpkin and other ingredients. They're typically fried until crispy on the outside and soft on the inside. These patties make a delicious vegetarian option and can be served with sour cream, yogurt, or a favorite dipping sauce for added flavor.

Ingredients (4 servings)
2 cups pumpkin, grated
1 small onion, finely chopped
2 cloves garlic, minced
½ cup all-purpose flour
2 eggs
1 teaspoon baking powder
1 teaspoon salt
½ teaspoon black pepper
½ teaspoon thyme, dried
¼ teaspoon ground nutmeg
¼ teaspoon paprika
Oil, for frying

Preparation
Place the grated pumpkin in a clean kitchen towel or cheesecloth, and squeeze out any excess moisture. In a suitable mixing bowl, mix the grated

pumpkin, chopped onion, minced garlic, flour, eggs, baking powder, salt, pepper, thyme, nutmeg, and paprika. Mix well to form a thick batter. Heat about ¼ inch of oil in a frying pan over medium heat. Drop spoonfuls of the pumpkin batter into the hot oil, and flatten them slightly with the back of a spoon to form patties. Fry the patties for 3-4 minutes on each side, until they are golden brown and crispy. Remove the patties from the pan and place them on a paper towel-lined plate to drain any excess oil. Repeat the process with the remaining batter, adding more oil to the pan, as needed. Serve the Estonian Kõrvitsakotletid hot as a side dish or a snack. Enjoy your delicious Estonian Pumpkin Patties!

Kama-Kotletid

Preparation time: 20 minutes
Cook time: 16 minutes
Nutrition facts (per serving): 314 Cal (17g fat, 4g protein, 1g fiber)

Kama is a traditional Estonian roasted grain flour mixture made from various grains, such as barley, rye, wheat, and peas. It's commonly used in Estonian cuisine to make porridges, desserts, and even savory dishes like these Kama-kotletid. These patties are a unique and tasty vegetarian option and can be served with sour cream, yogurt, or a favorite dipping sauce for added flavor.

Ingredients (4 servings)
1 cup Kama flour
1 small onion, finely chopped
2 cloves garlic, minced
2 small carrots, grated
1 small zucchini, grated
2 eggs
½ teaspoon salt
¼ teaspoon black pepper
½ teaspoon thyme, dried
½ teaspoon paprika
Oil, for frying

Preparation
In a suitable mixing bowl, mix the Kama flour, chopped onion, minced garlic, grated carrots, grated zucchini, eggs, salt, pepper, thyme, and

paprika. Mix well to form a thick batter. Heat about ¼ inch of oil in a frying pan over medium heat. Drop spoonfuls of the Kama batter into the hot oil, and flatten them slightly with the back of a spoon to form patties. Fry the patties for 3-4 minutes on each side, until they're golden brown and crispy. Remove the patties from the pan and place them on a paper towel-lined plate to drain any excess oil. Repeat the process with the remaining batter, adding more oil to the pan as needed. Serve the Estonian Kama-kotletid hot as a side dish or a snack. Enjoy your delicious Estonian Kama Patties!

Kapsarullid

Preparation time: 10 minutes
Cook time: 1 hour 30 minutes
Nutrition facts (per serving): 286 Cal (11g fat, 8g protein, 3g fiber)

Kapsarullid, Estonian cabbage rolls, are a savory and comforting dish made with cabbage leaves filled with a flavorful mixture of minced meat and rice, simmered in a tangy tomato sauce for a delicious and traditional meal that's loved by many in Estonian cuisine.

Ingredients (4 servings)
1 head of cabbage
1 cup cooked rice
1 small onion, finely chopped
2 cloves garlic, minced
½ pound ground meat (beef, pork, or a mixture)
½ teaspoon salt
¼ teaspoon black pepper
½ teaspoon thyme, dried
½ teaspoon paprika
1 egg
¼ cup bread crumbs
1 can (14 oz.) tomato sauce
¼ cup sour cream

Preparation
At 350°F, preheat your oven. Grease a baking dish and set aside. Bring a suitable pot of water to a boil. Remove the tough outer leaves from the

cabbage head and carefully separate the leaves. Blanch the cabbage leaves in boiling water for 2-3 minutes until pliable. Drain and set aside. In a suitable mixing bowl, mix the cooked rice, chopped onion, minced garlic, ground meat, salt, pepper, thyme, paprika, egg, and bread crumbs.

Mix well to form a filling. Place about 2-3 tablespoons of the meat filling onto each cabbage leaf and roll it up tightly, tucking in the sides as you go, like a burrito. Place the cabbage rolls seam-side down in the greased baking dish. In a separate bowl, mix together the tomato sauce and sour cream. Pour the tomato sauce mixture over the cabbage rolls. Cover the baking dish with aluminum foil and bake for 1 hour, until the cabbage rolls are tender and cooked through. Remove the foil and bake for an additional 10-15 minutes, until the sauce is slightly thickened and bubbly. Serve the Estonian Kapsarullid hot as a main course with a side of potatoes, rice, or salad. Enjoy your delicious Estonian Cabbage Rolls!

Kaalikapirukas

Preparation time: 10 minutes
Cook time: 46 minutes
Nutrition facts (per serving): 428 Cal (17g fat, 57g protein, 8g fiber)

Kaalikapirukas is a traditional Estonian dish often enjoyed during the colder months. It's a comforting and flavorful pie that features rutabaga, a root vegetable similar to turnip, as the main ingredient. The crust is typically buttery and flaky, and the filling is creamy and seasoned with herbs and spices. It can be served as a main dish or a side dish, and is perfect for gatherings and family meals.

Ingredients (4 servings)

Crust
1 and ¼ cups all-purpose flour
½ cup unsalted butter, chilled and diced
¼ teaspoon salt
4 tablespoons ice water

Filling
1 large rutabaga, peeled and diced
1 large onion, finely chopped
2 cloves garlic, minced
2 tablespoons butter
½ teaspoon salt
¼ teaspoon black pepper
½ teaspoon thyme, dried
½ teaspoon paprika

¼ cup all-purpose flour
1 and ¼ cups vegetable broth
½ cup heavy cream
¼ cup cheese (such as cheddar or Gouda), grated
Fresh parsley, chopped

Preparation
At 375°F, preheat your oven. Grease a pie dish and set aside. For the crust, in a suitable mixing bowl, whisk the flour and salt. Stir in the chilled diced butter and use a pastry cutter or your fingers to cut the butter into the flour until this mixture resembles coarse crumbs. Add ice water, one tablespoon at a time, and mix until this dough comes together. Form this dough into a ball, wrap it in plastic wrap, and refrigerate for 30 minutes.

Filling
In a suitable skillet, melt the butter over medium heat. Stir in the chopped onion and minced garlic and cook until softened, about 3-4 minutes. Stir in the diced rutabaga to the skillet and cook for another 5-7 minutes, stirring occasionally, until the rutabaga is slightly softened. Stir in the salt, pepper, dried thyme, and paprika. Drizzle the flour over the rutabaga mixture and stir to coat the vegetables. Gradually pour in the vegetable broth and heavy cream, stirring constantly, until this mixture thickens. Remove from heat and let the filling cool slightly.

On a floured surface, roll out the chilled dough into a circle large enough to fit the greased pie dish. Carefully transfer this dough to the pie dish and press it into the bottom and sides of the dish. Pour the rutabaga filling onto the crust in the pie dish. Drizzle grated cheese over the filling. Bake the Kaalikapirukas in the preheated oven for 30-35 minutes, until the crust is golden brown and the filling is bubbling. Remove from the oven and let the pie cool for a few minutes. Garnish with chopped fresh parsley before serving. Slice and serve the Estonian Kaalikapirukas as a delicious and hearty vegetarian main dish or side dish. Enjoy your tasty Rutabaga Pie!

Juurviljapada

Preparation time: 10 minutes
Cook time: 40 minutes
Nutrition facts (per serving): 442 Cal (37g fat, 11g protein, 0g fiber)

It's a comforting and nutritious stew that is perfect for colder weather, and it can be customized with your favorite vegetables and seasonings. It's typically served with bread or a side of sour cream, and makes a filling and delicious meal for vegetarians and vegans alike.

Ingredients (4 servings)
2 tablespoons butter or vegetable oil
1 large onion, chopped
3 cloves garlic, minced
2 carrots, peeled and diced
2 potatoes, peeled and diced
2 parsnips, peeled and diced
2 turnips, peeled and diced
½ small head of cabbage, shredded
1 bay leaf
1 teaspoon thyme, dried
1 teaspoon paprika
4 cups vegetable broth
Black pepper, to taste
Salt, to taste
Fresh parsley, chopped

Preparation

In a suitable pot, melt the butter or heat the vegetable oil over medium heat. Stir in the chopped onion and minced garlic to the pot and cook until the onion is translucent, about 5 minutes. Stir in the diced carrots, potatoes, parsnips, and turnips to the pot. Stir to coat the vegetables with the butter or oil. Stir in the shredded cabbage, bay leaf, dried thyme, and paprika to the pot. Stir to combine. Pour in the vegetable broth and bring this mixture to a boil.

Reduce the heat to low and let the stew simmer, covered, for about 30-40 minutes, until the vegetables are tender. Liberally season the stew with black pepper and salt to taste. Remove the bay leaf from the stew before serving. Ladle the hot Juurviljapada into serving bowls and garnish with chopped fresh parsley. Serve the Estonian Vegetable Stew as a satisfying and flavorful vegetarian main dish or side dish. Enjoy your delicious Juurviljapada!

Röstitud Juurviljad

Preparation time: 20 minutes
Cook time: 40 minutes
Nutrition facts (per serving): 295 Cal (28g fat, 3g protein, 2g fiber)

It's a versatile dish that can be served as a side dish to accompany meat or fish, or enjoyed on its own as a light and flavorful vegetarian meal. You can adjust the seasoning and cooking time to suit your taste preferences, and feel free to experiment with other root vegetables or herbs and spices to make it your own.

Ingredients (4 servings)
2 carrots, peeled and cut into sticks
2 parsnips, peeled and cut into sticks
2 potatoes, peeled and cut into chunks
1 onion, peeled and cut into wedges
2 tablespoons vegetable oil
1 teaspoon salt
½ teaspoon black pepper
1 teaspoon thyme, dried
1 teaspoon paprika
Fresh parsley, chopped

Preparation
At 400°F, preheat your oven and line a baking sheet with parchment paper. In a suitable mixing bowl, toss together the carrot sticks, parsnip sticks, potato chunks, and onion wedges with vegetable oil, salt, black pepper, dried thyme, and paprika until the vegetables are evenly coated

with the seasoning. Spread the seasoned vegetables in a single layer on the prepared baking sheet. Roast the vegetables in the preheated oven for about 30-40 minutes, until golden and crispy, stirring occasionally to ensure even cooking. Remove the roasted vegetables from the oven and transfer them to a serving dish. Garnish with chopped fresh parsley before serving. Serve the Estonian Röstitud Juurviljad as a delicious side dish or a light vegetarian main course. Enjoy your flavorful and crispy roasted vegetables!

Mushroom Stew (Seenehautis)

Preparation time: 15 minutes
Cook time: 33 minutes
Nutrition facts (per serving): 343 Cal (23g fat, 13g protein, 0.6g fiber)

Seenehautis, Estonian mushroom stew, is a rich and flavorful dish made with locally foraged mushrooms, onions, and cream, simmered together with aromatic spices for a delectable and comforting stew that's a beloved part of Estonian culinary heritage.

Ingredients (4 servings)
1 lb. fresh mushrooms, sliced
1 large onion, finely chopped
3 cloves garlic, minced
2 tablespoons butter
2 tablespoons all-purpose flour
1 ½ cups vegetable broth
⅔ cup heavy cream
1 tablespoon soy sauce
1 teaspoon thyme, dried
Black pepper, to taste
Salt, to taste
Fresh parsley, chopped

Preparation

In a suitable pot or Dutch oven, melt the butter over medium heat. Stir in the chopped onion and minced garlic, and sauté for 3-4 minutes, until the onion is soft and translucent. Stir in the sliced mushrooms to the pot and cook for another 5-7 minutes, until the mushrooms release their liquid and start to brown. Stir in the flour and cook for 1-2 minutes, stirring constantly, to form a roux. Gradually whisk in the vegetable broth, stirring constantly to avoid lumps. Stir in the dried thyme, soy sauce, salt, and pepper to the pot, and bring this mixture to a boil.

Reduce the heat to low and simmer for 10-15 minutes, until the stew thickens slightly. Stir in the heavy cream and simmer for another 5 minutes. Taste and adjust the seasoning, if needed. Remove the pot from the heat and let the mushroom stew cool slightly. Serve the Estonian Seenehautis hot, garnished with chopped fresh parsley. Enjoy your creamy and flavorful mushroom stew!

Rice and Chicken Casserole (Kana-Riisivorm)

Preparation time: 10 minutes
Cook time: 45 minutes
Nutrition facts (per serving): 478 Cal (26g fat, 24g protein, 2g fiber)

Kana-Riisivorm, Estonian rice and chicken casserole, is a comforting and wholesome dish made with tender chicken, fluffy rice, and creamy sauce, baked to perfection for a delicious and satisfying meal that's loved by families in Estonian cuisine.

Ingredients (4 servings)
1 cup uncooked white rice
2 cups chicken breast, cooked and diced
1 small onion, finely chopped
2 cloves garlic, minced
2 cups mixed vegetables (carrots, peas, corn), chopped
2 tablespoons butter
2 tablespoons all-purpose flour
2 cups chicken broth
1 cup milk
½ teaspoon salt, or to taste
¼ teaspoon black pepper, or to taste
½ cup cheese (cheddar or mozzarella), shredded
Fresh parsley, chopped (optional)

Preparation

Cook the rice according to package instructions and set aside. At 350°F, preheat your oven and grease a casserole dish. In a suitable skillet, melt the butter over medium heat. Stir in the chopped onion and minced garlic to the skillet and sauté for 2-3 minutes until softened. Stir in the mixed vegetables to the skillet and sauté for another 2-3 minutes until slightly tender. Stir in the flour and cook for 1-2 minutes until well combined. Gradually whisk in the chicken broth and milk, stirring constantly to avoid lumps.

Bring this mixture to a simmer and cook for 5-7 minutes until thickened, stirring frequently. Season with black pepper and salt to taste. Adjust the seasoning according to your preference. Stir in the cooked diced chicken and cooked rice, and mix well. Transfer this mixture to the prepared casserole dish and spread it evenly. Drizzle the shredded cheese on top of the casserole. Bake in the preheated oven for 25-30 minutes until bubbly and golden brown on top. Remove from the oven and leave it to cool for a few minutes before serving. Garnish with fresh chopped parsley, if desired. Serve hot and enjoy your Estonian Rice and Chicken Casserole!

Pajaroog

Preparation time: 10 minutes
Cook time: 2 hours 10 minutes
Nutrition facts (per serving): 338 Cal (10g fat, 33g protein, 3g fiber)

Pajaroog, Estonian beef casserole, is a hearty and flavorful dish made with tender beef, onions, and potatoes, baked to perfection for a comforting and delicious meal that is a popular favorite in Estonian cuisine.

Ingredients (4 servings)
1 lb. beef, cubed
1 large onion, finely chopped
2 carrots, peeled and diced
2 potatoes, peeled and diced
1 cup beef broth
1 cup heavy cream
2 tablespoons flour
2 tablespoons butter
2 tablespoons vegetable oil
Black pepper, to taste
Salt, to taste
Fresh parsley, for garnish

Preparation
At 350°F, preheat your oven. In a suitable oven-safe pot or casserole dish, heat the vegetable oil and butter over medium-high heat. Stir in the beef cubes and sear on all sides until browned. Remove the beef from the pot and set aside. In the same pot, stir in the chopped onion and carrots.

Cook until the vegetables are softened, about 5 minutes. Stir in the flour and cook for another 2-3 minutes, until the flour is lightly browned. Gradually whisk in the beef broth and heavy cream, stirring constantly to avoid lumps.

Stir in the diced potatoes and seared beef cubes back to the pot. Season with black pepper and salt to taste. Bring this mixture to a boil, then cover the pot with a lid and transfer to the preheated oven. Bake for about 1.5 to 2 hours, until the beef is tender and the vegetables are cooked through. Remove from the oven and let the casserole rest for a few minutes before serving. Garnish with fresh parsley, if desired, and serve hot.

Estonian Beef Meatballs (Lihapallid)

Preparation time: 10 minutes
Cook time: 14 minutes
Nutrition facts (per serving): 321 Cal (10g fat, 6.5g protein, 10g fiber)

Lihapallid, Estonian beef meatballs, are flavorful and juicy meatballs made with seasoned ground beef, onions, and spices, pan-fried to perfection for a delicious and comforting dish that's a staple in Estonian cuisine.

Ingredients (4 servings)
1 lb. ground beef
1 small onion, finely chopped
1 clove garlic, minced
1 egg
½ cup breadcrumbs
¼ cup milk
1 tablespoon fresh parsley, finely chopped
1 teaspoon salt
½ teaspoon black pepper
½ teaspoon paprika
¼ teaspoon ground allspice
¼ teaspoon ground nutmeg
2 tablespoons vegetable oil, for frying

Preparation

In a suitable mixing bowl, mix the ground beef, chopped onion, minced the garlic, egg, breadcrumbs, milk, parsley, salt, pepper, paprika, allspice, and nutmeg. Mix well until all the ingredients are thoroughly combined. Shape this mixture into small meatballs using your hands. In a suitable skillet, heat the vegetable oil over medium heat. Stir in the meatballs to the skillet and cook for about 5-7 minutes, turning occasionally, until they are browned on all sides and cooked through. Once the meatballs are cooked, remove them from the skillet and place them on a paper towel-lined plate to absorb any excess oil. Serve the Estonian beef meatballs hot with your favorite side dish, such as mashed potatoes, rice, or vegetables.

Estonian Beef Roulades (Räimerullid)

Preparation time: 15 minutes
Cook time: 25 minutes
Nutrition facts (per serving): 478 Cal (11g fat, 55g protein, 3g fiber)

Räimerullid, Estonian beef roulades, are succulent beef rolls filled with a flavorful mixture of onions, bacon, and pickles, simmered in a savory sauce for a delectable and hearty dish that's a favorite in Estonian cuisine.

Ingredients (2 servings)
4 thin beef slices (flank steak or sirloin), about 8 oz. each
4 slices bacon
1 small onion, finely chopped
1 clove garlic, minced
2 tablespoons vegetable oil
2 tablespoons Dijon mustard
4 small pickles (gherkins), halved lengthwise
Black pepper, to taste
Salt, to taste

Preparation
Lay out the beef slices on a flat surface and season with black pepper and salt to taste. In a suitable skillet, heat the vegetable oil over medium heat. Stir in the chopped onion and minced garlic, and sauté until softened, about 3-4 minutes. Place a slice of bacon, a suitable spoonful of sautéed onion and garlic mixture, and half a pickle on top of each beef slice. Roll

up the beef slices tightly, tucking in the sides as you go, and secure with toothpicks to hold the roulades together. Heat a suitable skillet over medium-high heat. Add a little vegetable oil, if needed.

Carefully place the beef roulades in the hot skillet and sear on all sides until browned, about 2-3 minutes per side. Reduce the heat to low and continue to cook the roulades for another 10-15 minutes, turning occasionally, until cooked to your desired level of doneness. Remove the beef roulades from the skillet and let them rest for a few minutes before removing the toothpicks and slicing them crosswise into rounds. Serve the Estonian beef roulades hot with your favorite side dish, such as roasted potatoes, steamed vegetables, or mashed potatoes.

Estonian Beef Patties (Hakklihakotletid)

Preparation time: 10 minutes
Cook time: 14 minutes
Nutrition facts (per serving): 391 Cal (27g fat, 27g protein, 2g fiber)

Hakklihakotletid, Estonian beef patties, are deliciously seasoned ground beef patties that are pan-fried to perfection, resulting in juicy and flavorful meat patties that are a beloved classic in Estonian cuisine.

Ingredients (4 servings)
1 lb. ground beef
1 small onion, finely chopped
2 cloves garlic, minced
1 egg
½ cup bread crumbs
½ teaspoon salt
¼ teaspoon black pepper
¼ teaspoon paprika
2 tablespoons vegetable oil, for frying

Preparation
In a suitable mixing bowl, mix the ground beef, chopped onion, minced garlic, egg, bread crumbs, salt, black pepper, and paprika. Mix well until all the ingredients are evenly incorporated. Shape the beef mixture into patties, about 2-3 inches in diameter and ½ inch thick. Heat the vegetable oil in a frying pan over medium heat. Stir in the beef patties to the hot

pan and cook for 3-4 minutes per side, until they are cooked through and have a golden crust on the outside. Transfer the cooked beef patties to a paper towel-lined plate to drain off any excess oil. Serve the Estonian beef patties hot with your favorite side dish, such as mashed potatoes, steamed vegetables, or a fresh salad.

Estonian Rolled Herring (Räimerullid)

Preparation time: 10 minutes
Nutrition facts (per serving): 296 Cal (7g fat, 17g protein, 4g fiber)

Räimerullid, Estonian rolled herring, are a traditional dish made with pickled herring fillets rolled with a tasty filling of onions, carrots, and spices, creating a flavorful and tangy treat that is popular in Estonian cuisine.

Ingredients (4 servings)
8 pickled herring fillets
8 small boiled potatoes
1 small red onion, finely chopped
1 tablespoon fresh dill, chopped
1 tablespoon sour cream or mayonnaise
Black pepper, to taste
Salt, to taste

Preparation
Rinse the pickled herring fillets under cold water to remove excess brine. Pat dry with paper towels. In a suitable bowl, mix together the chopped red onion, fresh dill, sour cream or mayonnaise, black pepper and salt. Lay out the herring fillets on a clean surface, with the skin side facing down. Place a suitable boiled potato on each herring fillet and spread a suitable amount of the onion and dill mixture on top of the potato. Roll up the herring fillets with the potato and filling inside, securing with a

toothpick, if needed. Arrange the herring rolls on a serving plate and refrigerate for at least 1 hour before serving to allow the flavors to meld together. Serve the Estonian herring rolls as an appetizer, garnished with additional fresh dill, if desired.

Beef and Potato Casserole

Preparation time: 20 minutes
Cook time: 62 minutes
Nutrition facts (per serving): 292 Cal (13g fat, 41g protein, 0.5g fiber)

This Estonian Beef and Potato Casserole is a flavorful and satisfying dish that is perfect for colder weather or when you're craving a hearty and comforting meal. Enjoy this traditional Estonian recipe!

Ingredients (4 servings)
1 lb. beef stew meat, cubed
4 medium potatoes, peeled and thinly sliced
1 large onion, finely chopped
2 cloves garlic, minced
2 tablespoons vegetable oil
2 tablespoons all-purpose flour
2 cups beef broth
1 cup sour cream
1 teaspoon paprika
½ teaspoon salt
¼ teaspoon black pepper
Chopped fresh parsley, for garnish

Preparation
At 350°F, preheat your oven. In a suitable oven-safe casserole dish or Dutch oven, heat the vegetable oil over medium heat. Stir in the chopped onion and minced garlic, and sauté until softened, about 3-4 minutes. Stir in the cubed beef stew meat to the casserole dish, and cook until

browned on all sides, about 5-7 minutes. Remove the beef from the casserole dish and set aside. In the same casserole dish, stir in the flour and cook for 1-2 minutes, stirring constantly, until lightly golden.

Gradually whisk in the beef broth, scraping up any browned bits from the bottom of the casserole dish. Bring to a boil and cook for 2-3 minutes, until the sauce thickens slightly. Stir in the sour cream, paprika, black pepper and salt until well combined. Stir in the sliced potatoes and browned beef back into the casserole dish, stirring to coat them with the sauce. Cover the casserole dish with a lid or aluminum foil and transfer it to the preheated oven. Bake for 45-50 minutes, until the potatoes are tender and the beef is cooked through. Remove the casserole from the oven and let it rest for a few minutes before serving. Garnish with chopped fresh parsley before serving.

Marmorliha

Preparation time: 10 minutes
Cook time: 15 minutes
Nutrition facts (per serving): 308 Cal (10g fat, 44g protein, 0.4g fiber)

Marmorliha, or Estonian Beef Marble Meat, is a classic dish in Estonian cuisine that features tender beef cooked in a creamy sauce with a marbled appearance.

Ingredients (4 servings)
1 lb. beef steak, thinly sliced
1 large onion, finely chopped
2 cloves garlic, minced
2 tablespoons butter
2 tablespoons all-purpose flour
2 cups beef broth
1 cup heavy cream
1 tablespoon Worcestershire sauce
1 tablespoon Dijon mustard
Black pepper, to taste
Salt, to taste
Fresh parsley, for garnish

Preparation
Heat a suitable skillet over medium-high heat and melt the butter. Stir in the sliced beef to the skillet and cook until browned on both sides, about 2-3 minutes per side. Remove the beef from the skillet and set aside. In the same skillet, stir in the chopped onion and minced garlic, and sauté

until softened, about 3-4 minutes. Stir in the flour and cook for 1-2 minutes, stirring constantly, until lightly golden.

Gradually whisk in the beef broth, scraping up any browned bits from the bottom of the skillet. Bring to a boil and cook for 2-3 minutes, until the sauce thickens slightly. Stir in the heavy cream, Worcestershire sauce, and Dijon mustard until well combined. Season with black pepper and salt to taste. Return the cooked beef slices to the skillet, and cook for an additional 5-7 minutes, until the beef is cooked through and the sauce has thickened to your desired consistency. Remove the skillet from the heat and let it rest for a few minutes before serving. Garnish with chopped fresh parsley before serving.

Chicken Pate

Indulge in the rich and savory flavor of Chicken Pate, a delectable spread perfect for gourmet appetizers.

Preparation time: 10 minutes
Cook time: 35 minutes
Nutrition facts (per serving): 324 Cal (16g fat, 13g protein, 3g fiber)

Ingredients (4 servings)
1 lb. boneless, skinless chicken breasts or thighs
1 medium onion, finely chopped
2 cloves garlic, minced
3 ½ oz. butter, softened
2 tablespoons all-purpose flour
½ cup chicken broth
½ cup heavy cream
Black pepper, to taste
Salt, to taste
Fresh herbs (parsley or thyme), for garnish

Preparation
At 350°F, preheat your oven. In a suitable saucepan, melt 1 oz. of butter over medium heat. Stir in the chopped onion and minced garlic and sauté until softened, about 3-4 minutes. Stir in the chicken pieces to the saucepan and cook until they are no longer pink, about 5-6 minutes. Remove the saucepan from the heat and let the chicken mixture cool slightly. Once the chicken mixture has cooled, transfer it to a food processor or blender. Stir in the softened butter and flour to the food

processor or blender and process until smooth. Return the chicken mixture to the saucepan and place it back on the stove over medium heat.

Gradually stir in the chicken broth and heavy cream, whisking constantly to avoid lumps. Cook this mixture, stirring frequently, until it thickens, about 5 minutes. Liberally season the chicken pate with black pepper and salt to taste. Pour the chicken pate into a greased baking dish or individual ramekins. Bake in the preheated oven for 20-25 minutes, until the top is lightly golden brown and the pate is set. Remove from the oven and leave it to cool to room temperature.

Once cooled, cover with plastic wrap and refrigerate for at least 2-3 hours until the pate is firm. Before serving, garnish with fresh herbs, such as parsley or thyme, if desired. Serve the Estonian Chicken Pate with crackers, bread, or toast points as an appetizer or snack. Enjoy your homemade Estonian Chicken Pate!

Chicken and Pasta Casserole

Enjoy a comforting and satisfying meal with Chicken and Pasta Casserole, a flavorful combination of tender chicken, al dente pasta, and cheesy goodness, baked to perfection.

Preparation time: 15 minutes
Cook time: 38 minutes
Nutrition facts (per serving): 557 Cal (19g fat, 33g protein, 5g fiber)

Ingredients (4 servings)
1 lb. boneless, skinless chicken breasts or thighs, diced
9 oz. pasta (macaroni, fusilli, or penne)
1 medium onion, finely chopped
2 cloves garlic, minced
2 tablespoons butter
2 tablespoons all-purpose flour
2 cups chicken broth
1 cup heavy cream
1 cup cheese (cheddar or mozzarella), shredded
½ teaspoon thyme, dried
Black pepper, to taste
Salt, to taste
Fresh parsley, for garnish

Preparation
At 350°F, preheat your oven and grease a 9 x 13 inch baking dish. Cook the pasta according to package instructions until al dente. Drain and set aside. In a suitable skillet, melt the butter over medium heat. Stir in the

chopped onion and minced garlic and sauté until softened, about 3-4 minutes. Stir in the diced chicken to the skillet and cook until it's no longer pink, about 5-6 minutes. Stir in the flour and cook for another 1-2 minutes, until it's lightly golden brown.

Gradually whisk in the chicken broth and heavy cream, stirring constantly to avoid lumps. Cook this mixture, stirring frequently, until it thickens, about 5 minutes. Stir in the shredded cheese, dried thyme, salt, and pepper. Continue stirring until the cheese is melted and the sauce is smooth. Remove the skillet from the heat and stir in the cooked pasta until evenly coated with the sauce. Transfer this mixture to the greased baking dish and spread it out in an even layer. Bake in the preheated oven for 20-25 minutes, until the top is golden and bubbly. Remove from the oven and leave it to cool for a few minutes before serving. Garnish with fresh parsley, if desired, before serving. Enjoy your delicious Estonian Chicken and Pasta Casserole!

Estonian Chicken Wraps (Kanawrapid)

Savor the unique taste of Kanawrapid, Estonian-style Chicken Wraps, featuring succulent marinated chicken wrapped in soft flatbread and served with a delightful blend of herbs and sauces.

Preparation time: 20 minutes
Cook time: 16 minutes
Nutrition facts (per serving): 308 Cal (10g fat, 44g protein, 0.4g fiber)

Ingredients (2 servings)
1 lb. boneless, skinless chicken breasts, thinly sliced
1 large onion, thinly sliced
1 large bell pepper, thinly sliced
2 cloves garlic, minced
2 tablespoons vegetable oil
1 tablespoon soy sauce
1 tablespoon Worcestershire sauce
1 teaspoon paprika
Black pepper, to taste
Salt, to taste
Tortilla wraps or thin flatbreads
Lettuce leaves, for wrapping (optional)

Preparation
In a suitable skillet, heat the vegetable oil over medium-high heat. Stir in the thinly sliced chicken breasts and cook until they're no longer pink and

are cooked through, about 5-6 minutes. Remove from the skillet and set aside. In the same skillet, add a little more oil, if needed, and then stir in the sliced onion, bell pepper, and minced garlic. Sauté until the vegetables are softened, about 3-4 minutes. Stir in the cooked chicken back to the skillet with the sautéed vegetables. Stir in the soy sauce, Worcestershire sauce, paprika, salt, and pepper.

Cook for another 2-3 minutes, stirring occasionally, to allow the flavors to meld. Remove from heat and let the chicken and vegetable mixture cool slightly. Warm up the tortilla wraps or thin flatbreads according to package instructions. Place a scoop of the chicken and vegetable mixture onto each tortilla wrap or flatbread. If desired, add lettuce leaves on top of the chicken and vegetable mixture for extra crunch and freshness. Wrap up the tortilla or flatbread, tucking in the sides as you go. Serve immediately and enjoy your delicious Estonian Chicken Wraps!

Grilled Pork Chops (Grillitud Seakarbonaad)

Preparation time: 10 minutes
Cook time: 12 minutes
Nutrition facts (per serving): 292 Cal (13g fat, 41g protein, 0.5g fiber)

Estonian grilled pork chops, known as "Grillitud Seakarbonaad" in Estonian, are succulent and tender pork chops marinated in a flavorful blend of herbs and spices, then grilled to perfection for a delicious and satisfying dish that's a favorite in Estonian cuisine.

Ingredients (4 servings)
5 pork chops
¼ cup vegetable oil
¼ cup white wine vinegar
1 teaspoon salt
½ teaspoon black pepper

Preparation
In a suitable bowl, whisk vegetable oil, white wine vinegar, black pepper and salt to make the marinade. Place the pork chops in a shallow dish and pour the marinade over them, making sure each chop is coated well. Cover the dish with plastic wrap and let the pork chops marinate in the refrigerator for at least 30 minutes, or overnight for best results. Preheat your barbecue or grill to medium-high heat. Remove the pork chops from the marinade and shake off excess marinade. Place the pork chops on the preheated grill and grill for about 5-6 minutes per side, until they

are cooked through and have grill marks. Remove the pork chops from the grill and let them rest for a few minutes before serving. Serve hot with your favorite side dishes or condiments, and enjoy your Estonian Grilled Pork Chops!

Beef and Vegetable Skewers (Veiseliha- ja Köögiviljavardad)

Preparation time: 10 minutes
Cook time: 10 minutes
Nutrition facts (per serving): 432 Cal (14g fat, 30g protein, 1.3g fiber)

Estonian beef and vegetable skewers, or "Veiseliha- ja Köögiviljavardad" in Estonian, are a delicious combination of marinated beef chunks and fresh vegetables, grilled to perfection for a flavorful and satisfying dish that's popular in Estonian cuisine.

Ingredients (4 servings)
2 lb. beef sirloin or tenderloin, cut into chunks
1 bell pepper, cut into chunks
1 red onion, cut into chunks
6 cherry tomatoes
2 tablespoons olive oil
1 tablespoon red wine vinegar
1 teaspoon fresh rosemary, chopped
Black pepper, to taste
Salt, to taste

Preparation
Thread the beef, bell peppers, red onion, and cherry tomatoes onto the skewers, alternating the pieces. In a suitable bowl, whisk olive oil, red wine vinegar, rosemary, salt, and pepper to make a marinade. Brush the marinade over the skewers. Grill the skewers on a barbecue or grill for

about 8-10 minutes, turning occasionally, until the beef is cooked to your desired level of doneness. Serve hot and enjoy!

Veggie and Halloumi Skewers

Preparation time: 10 minutes
Cook time: 8 minutes
Nutrition facts (per serving): 259 Cal (5 g fat, 23g protein, 6g fiber)

Estonian veggie and halloumi skewers, or "Köögivilja- ja Halloumivardad" in Estonian, are a delightful combination of marinated vegetables and halloumi cheese, grilled to perfection for a delicious and wholesome dish that's loved in Estonian cuisine.

Ingredients (4 servings)
1 lb. assorted vegetables (bell peppers, zucchini, mushrooms, cherry tomatoes)
½ lb. halloumi cheese, cut into chunks
2 tablespoons olive oil
1 tablespoon lemon juice
Fresh oregano, chopped
Black pepper, to taste
Salt, to taste

Preparation
Thread the vegetables and halloumi cheese onto the skewers, alternating the pieces. In a suitable bowl, whisk olive oil, lemon juice, oregano, salt, and pepper to make a marinade. Brush the marinade over the skewers. Grill the skewers on a barbecue or grill for about 6-8 minutes, turning occasionally, until the vegetables are tender and the halloumi cheese is slightly golden. Serve hot and enjoy!

Dessert

Sweet Braided Bread

Preparation time: 15 minutes
Cook time: 30 minutes
Nutrition facts (per serving): 367 Cal (21g fat, 9g protein, 1.2g fiber)

An Estonian sweet braided bread, is a traditional treat with a soft, fluffy texture and a delightful hint of cardamom, often enjoyed during special occasions and celebrations in Estonia.

Ingredients (8 servings)
Dough
1 lb. all-purpose flour
1 packet active dry yeast
1 cup milk
3 ½ oz. unsalted butter, melted
3 ½ oz. sugar, granulated
2 large eggs
1 teaspoon vanilla extract
½ teaspoon salt

Filling
1 ½ oz. unsalted butter, softened
3 ½ oz. sugar, granulated
2 teaspoons ground cinnamon

Glaze
1 egg, beaten
Pearl sugar (optional)

Preparation

In a suitable mixing bowl, mix the flour and yeast. In a saucepan, heat the milk until warm, then whisk in the melted butter, sugar, eggs, vanilla extract, and salt. Stir in the milk mixture to the flour mixture and stir until a dough forms. Knead this dough on a floured surface for about 5 minutes, then place it back in the bowl, cover with a clean towel, and let it rise for 1 hour, until doubled in size.

At 350°F, preheat your oven and line a baking sheet with parchment paper. Punch down this dough and turn it out onto a floured surface. Roll it into a suitable rectangle.

For the filling, mix together the softened butter, sugar, and cinnamon, then spread it evenly over this dough. Roll up this dough tightly from the long edge, then transfer it to the prepared baking sheet and shape it into a ring. Use a pair of kitchen shears or a sharp knife to make cuts around the ring at regular intervals, leaving about 1 inch of dough intact at the center. Twist each section of dough outward to reveal the filling, then brush this dough with the beaten egg and drizzle with pearl sugar, if desired.

Bake in the preheated oven for 25-30 minutes, until golden brown. Remove from the oven and leave it to cool slightly before serving. Enjoy your homemade Estonian Kringel!

Estonian Curd Cake (Kohupiimakook)

Preparation time: 20 minutes
Cook time: 45 minutes
Nutrition facts (per serving): 265 Cal (5g fat, 7g protein, 5g fiber)

Kohupiimakook, an Estonian curd cake, is a luscious and creamy dessert made with fresh curd cheese, eggs, and sugar, often topped with a sweet glaze or fresh berries for a delightful treat.

Ingredients (8 servings)
Crust
8 oz. digestive biscuits or graham crackers
3 ½ oz. unsalted butter, melted

Filling
1 lb. Estonian curd cheese (kohupiim)
⅔ cup sour cream
⅔ cup heavy cream
4 oz. sugar, granulated
4 large eggs
2 teaspoons vanilla extract
Zest of 1 lemon (optional)

Topping
Fresh berries (strawberries, blueberries, raspberries)
Fruit preserves (strawberry or raspberry preserves)

Preparation

At 350°F, preheat your oven and grease a 9-inch springform pan. Crush the digestive biscuits or graham crackers into fine crumbs and mix them with the melted butter until well combined. Press this mixture firmly into the bottom of the prepared springform pan to form the crust.

In a suitable mixing bowl, whisk the curd cheese, sour cream, heavy cream, sugar, eggs, vanilla extract, and lemon zest (if using) until smooth and well combined. Pour the curd cheese filling over the crust in the springform pan. Bake in the preheated oven for 40-45 minutes, until the edges are set and the center is slightly jiggly. Turn off the oven and crack the oven door open slightly. Let the cake cool in the oven for about 1 hour, then remove from the oven and leave it to cool completely at room temperature.

Once cooled, refrigerate the cake for at least 4 hours, or preferably overnight, to allow it to set completely. Just before serving, remove the cake from the springform pan and transfer it to a serving plate. Top the cake with fresh berries or fruit preserves, and optionally, dust with powdered sugar. Slice and serve chilled. Enjoy your delicious Estonian Kohupiimakook!

Rye Bread Cake (Karask)

Preparation time: 20 minutes
Cook time: 30 minutes
Nutrition facts (per serving): 221 Cal (11g fat, 4g protein, 1.4g fiber)

Karask, an Estonian rye bread cake, is a traditional dessert made with hearty rye bread, rich butter, and sweet ingredients like honey, dried fruits, and spices, resulting in a dense and delicious treat with a distinctively rustic flavor.

Ingredients (8 servings)
9 oz. rye flour
3 ½ oz. all-purpose flour
1 teaspoon baking soda
1 teaspoon salt
1 tablespoon sugar
1 cup buttermilk
2 tablespoons molasses or dark syrup
2 tablespoons vegetable oil
1 large egg

Preparation
At 400°F, preheat your oven and grease a round cake pan or cast iron skillet. In a suitable mixing bowl, whisk the rye flour, all-purpose flour, baking soda, salt, and sugar. In a separate bowl, whisk the buttermilk, molasses or dark syrup, vegetable oil, and egg. Gradually pour the wet

ingredients into the dry ingredients, stirring until a thick batter forms. Pour the prepared batter into the prepared cake pan or skillet, spreading it out evenly.

Bake in the preheated oven for 25-30 minutes, until a toothpick inserted into the center comes out clean. Remove from the oven and let the Karask cool in the pan or skillet for a few minutes, then place it onto the wire rack to cool completely. Once cooled, you can optionally serve the Karask with butter or other toppings, such as cheese or cured fish. Slice and enjoy your delicious Estonian Karask, a unique rye bread cake that's perfect for breakfast or as a snack!

Teddy Bear Cake (Mõmmik)

Preparation time: 20 minutes
Cook time: 35 minutes
Nutrition facts (per serving): 317 Cal (17g fat, 5g protein, 0.8g fiber)

Mõmmik, a Teddy Bear Cake, is a delightful dessert shaped like a cuddly teddy bear, typically made with layers of moist sponge cake, sweet cream, and colorful decorations, perfect for kids' birthdays or special occasions.

Ingredients (8 servings)
Cake
8 oz. unsalted butter, at room temperature
8 oz. granulated sugar
4 large eggs
8 oz. all-purpose flour
2 teaspoons baking powder
¼ teaspoon salt
1 teaspoon vanilla extract
½ cup milk

Filling
1 ¼ cup heavy cream
8 oz. chocolate (dark or milk), chopped
3 ½ oz. unsalted butter, at room temperature
2 tablespoons powdered sugar
1 teaspoon vanilla extract

Decoration

Fondant icing (brown, black, white, and any other desired colors)
Food coloring (optional)
Candy or chocolate decorations (M&M's, gummy bears or chocolate chips)
Edible glue or water for sticking the decorations

Preparation

Cake

At 350°F, preheat your oven and grease and flour a Teddy Bear-shaped cake pan or a regular round cake pan. In a suitable mixing bowl, cream together the butter and sugar until light and fluffy. Stir in the eggs, one by one, and beat well after each addition. In a separate bowl, whisk the flour, baking powder, and salt. Gradually stir in the dry ingredients to the butter mixture, alternating with the milk and vanilla extract, beginning and ending with the dry ingredients. Mix until just combined. Pour the cake batter into the prepared cake pan and spread it out evenly. Bake in the preheated oven for 30-35 minutes, until a toothpick inserted into the center comes out clean. Remove from the oven and let the cake cool in the pan for 10 minutes, then place it onto the wire rack to cool completely.

Filling

In a heatproof bowl, mix the chopped chocolate and butter. In a saucepan, heat the heavy cream over medium heat until it just begins to boil. Pour the hot cream over the chocolate and butter mixture and let it sit for a minute. Stir this mixture until the chocolate and butter are completely melted and smooth. Stir in the powdered sugar and vanilla extract, and whisk until well combined. Let the filling cool to room temperature, then cover and refrigerate for at least 2 hours, until thickened and spreadable.

Assembly and Decoration

Once the cake and filling are completely cooled, you can begin assembling and decorating your Teddy Bear Cake. If necessary, trim the top of the cake to make it level. Cut the cake horizontally into two layers. Place one cake layer on a serving plate and spread a thick layer of the chilled chocolate filling on top. Place the second cake layer on top of the filling. Use a sharp knife to shape the cake into a Teddy Bear shape, if using a regular round cake pan. Roll out brown fondant icing and cover the entire cake, using your hands or a rolling pin to smooth it out and shape it to resemble a Teddy Bear. Roll out other colored fondant icing to create the eyes, nose, mouth, and other desired decorations for the Teddy Bear's face and body. You can also use food coloring to color the fondant. Use edible glue or water to stick the fondant decorations onto the cake, creating the Teddy Bear's face and body, as desired.

Quark Cheese Cake (Kubujuustukook)

Preparation time: 15 minutes
Cook time: 40 minutes
Nutrition facts (per serving): 202 Cal (7g fat, 6g protein, 1.3g fiber)

Kubujuustukook, also known as Estonian Quark Cheese Cake, is a popular dessert in Estonia. It's a creamy and delicious cake made with quark cheese, a type of fresh cheese, and is typically served chilled.

Ingredients (8 servings)
Crust
9 oz. digestive biscuits or graham crackers
3 ½ oz. unsalted butter, melted

Filling
1 lb. quark cheese (sometimes called curd cheese or farmer cheese), drained
8 oz. sugar, granulated
4 large eggs
⅔ cup heavy cream
1 teaspoon vanilla extract
Zest of 1 lemon

Topping
Fresh berries or fruit of your choice (strawberries, blueberries or raspberries)
Powdered sugar, for dusting (optional)

Preparation

Crust

Crush the digestive biscuits or graham crackers into fine crumbs using a food processor or by placing them in a plastic bag and using a rolling pin. In a suitable mixing bowl, mix the biscuit or cracker crumbs with the melted butter and mix well. Press this mixture firmly into the bottom of a 9-inch springform pan to form the crust. Place the pan in the refrigerator to chill while you prepare the filling.

Filling

At 350°F, preheat your oven. In a suitable mixing bowl, mix the quark cheese and sugar, and mix well. Stir in the eggs, one by one, and beat well after each addition. Stir in the heavy cream, vanilla extract, and lemon zest, and mix until well combined. Pour the filling over the chilled crust in the springform pan, spreading it out evenly. Bake in the preheated oven for 35-40 minutes, until the edges are set and the center is slightly jiggly. Remove from the oven and let the cake cool in the pan for 10 minutes, then run a knife around the edges to loosen it from the pan.

Transfer the cake to a wire rack to cool completely, then cover and refrigerate for at least 4 hours or overnight to set. For the topping: Just before serving, decorate the chilled quark cheese cake with fresh berries or fruit of your choice on top. Dust with powdered sugar, if desired, for a decorative finish. Slice and serve the chilled Kubujuustukook, and enjoy this creamy and delicious Estonian Quark Cheese Cake with its rich flavors and refreshing fruit topping!

Grandma's Cake (Vanaema Kook)

Preparation time: 15 minutes
Cook time: 35 minutes
Nutrition facts (per serving): 393 Cal (18g g fat, 9g protein, 3g fiber)

Vanaema Kook, or Estonian Grandma's Cake, is a traditional dessert in Estonia that has a nostalgic and comforting taste. It's a simple yet delicious cake made with a sweet biscuit crust and a rich and creamy filling.

Ingredients (8 servings)

Crust

9 oz. digestive biscuits or graham crackers
3 ½ oz. unsalted butter, melted
1 tablespoon cocoa powder (optional)

Filling

4 large eggs
8 oz. sugar, granulated
⅔ cup heavy cream
2 teaspoons vanilla extract
2 tablespoons all-purpose flour
¼ teaspoon salt
Zest of 1 lemon

Preparation

Crust

Crush the digestive biscuits or graham crackers into fine crumbs using a food processor or by placing them in a plastic bag and using a rolling pin. In a suitable mixing bowl, mix the biscuit or cracker crumbs with the melted butter and cocoa powder (if using), and mix well. Press this mixture firmly into the bottom of a 9-inch springform pan to form the crust. Place the pan in the refrigerator to chill while you prepare the filling.

Filling

At 350°F, preheat your oven. In a suitable mixing bowl, beat the eggs and sugar together until light and fluffy. Stir in the heavy cream, vanilla extract, flour, salt, and lemon zest, and mix until well combined. Pour the filling over the chilled crust in the springform pan, spreading it out evenly. Bake in the preheated oven for 30-35 minutes, until the edges are set and the center is slightly jiggly. Remove from the oven and let the cake cool in the pan for 10 minutes, then run a knife around the edges to loosen it from the pan.

Transfer the cake to a wire rack to cool completely, then cover and refrigerate for at least 4 hours or overnight to set. Slice and serve the chilled Vanaema Kook, and enjoy this nostalgic Estonian Grandma's Cake with its simple yet delightful flavors!

Estonian Sheet Cake (Plaadikook)

Preparation time: 15 minutes
Cook time: 25 minutes
Nutrition facts (per serving): 181 Cal (6g fat, 2.4g protein, 0.6g fiber)

Plaadikook, or Estonian Sheet Cake, is a delicious and popular dessert in Estonia that's often served at special occasions and festive celebrations. It's a simple yet scrumptious cake made with a tender sponge cake base and a sweet vanilla cream topping.

Ingredients (8 servings)
Sponge Cake Base
4 large eggs
8 oz. sugar, granulated
8 oz. all-purpose flour
1 teaspoon baking powder
¼ teaspoon salt
2 teaspoons vanilla extract

Cream Topping
2 cups heavy cream
8 oz. sugar, granulated
2 tablespoons all-purpose flour
2 tablespoons cornstarch
1 teaspoon vanilla extract

Preparation

Sponge Cake Base

At 350°F, preheat your oven and grease a 9 x 13 inch baking sheet or rectangular cake pan. In a suitable mixing bowl, beat the eggs and sugar together until light and fluffy. Stir in the flour, baking powder, salt, and vanilla extract, and mix until well combined. Pour the prepared batter into the prepared baking sheet or cake pan, spreading it out evenly. Bake in the preheated oven for 20-25 minutes, until the cake is golden brown and a toothpick inserted into the center comes out clean. Remove from the oven and let the cake cool completely in the pan.

Cream Topping

In a saucepan, mix the heavy cream, sugar, flour, and cornstarch. Whisk until well combined. Place the saucepan over medium heat and cook, stirring constantly, until this mixture thickens and comes to a boil. Remove from the heat and stir in the vanilla extract. Let the cream topping cool slightly, then pour it over the cooled sponge cake base in the baking sheet or cake pan, spreading it out evenly with a spatula.

Refrigerate the Paladion for at least 4 hours or overnight to set the cream topping. Slice and serve the chilled Paladion, and enjoy this delightful Estonian Sheet Cake with its soft sponge cake base and creamy vanilla topping!

Raisin Kissel (Rosinakissell)

Preparation time: 15 minutes
Cook time: 20 minutes
Nutrition facts (per serving): 101 Cal (7g fat, 1.3g protein, 1g fiber)

Rosinakissell, or Estonian Raisin Kissel, is a traditional dessert in Estonia that is often enjoyed during the holiday season or as a refreshing summer treat. It's a sweet and tangy dessert made with raisins and a thickened berry juice or fruit compote.

Ingredients (8 servings)

4 oz. raisins
2 cups water
9 oz. fresh or frozen berries (such as lingonberries, raspberries, or blackcurrants)
3 ½ oz. sugar, granulated
2 tablespoons cornstarch or potato starch
2 tablespoons cold water
1 teaspoon lemon juice (optional)

Preparation

Place the raisins in a saucepan with 2 cups of water and bring to a boil. Reduce its heat and simmer for 10-15 minutes, until the raisins are plump and soft. In a separate saucepan, mix the berries and sugar. Cook over medium heat, stirring occasionally, until the berries release their juices and the sugar is dissolved. In a suitable bowl, whisk the cornstarch or potato starch with 2 tablespoons of cold water until smooth. Gradually stir the cornstarch or potato starch mixture into the berry mixture, whisking constantly to prevent lumps from forming.

Continue to cook this mixture over low heat, stirring constantly, until it thickens to a jelly-like consistency. Remove from heat and stir in the cooked raisins and lemon juice (if using).Let the Rosinakissell cool slightly, then transfer to serving bowls or glasses. Refrigerate for at least 2-3 hours, until the kissel is chilled and set. Serve the chilled Rosinakissell as a refreshing and tangy dessert, and enjoy the burst of flavor from the juicy raisins and sweet berry compote. It's a delightful Estonian dessert that's perfect for special occasions or any time you're craving a sweet treat with a touch of tartness!

Estonian Dessert Soup (Leivasupp)

Preparation time: 20 minutes
Cook time: 17 minutes
Nutrition facts (per serving): 374 Cal (14g fat, 7g protein, 2g fiber)

Leivasupp, or Estonian Bread Soup, is a traditional dessert soup in Estonia that's often enjoyed during the winter months or as a comforting treat. It's made with simple ingredients like rye bread, water, and sweeteners such as sugar or honey, and it's often spiced with warming flavors like cinnamon and cardamom.

Ingredients (4 servings)
9 oz. rye bread (preferably stale or day-old)
4 ¼ cups water
3 ½ oz. granulated sugar or to taste
1 cinnamon stick
3-4 whole cardamom pods
1 tablespoon butter
1 tablespoon all-purpose flour
1 tablespoon cocoa powder (optional)
½ teaspoon salt
Whipped cream, for garnish (optional)

Preparation
Cut the rye bread into small cubes or slices and place them in a suitable saucepan or pot. Stir in the water to the saucepan with the bread, and

bring to a boil over medium heat. Reduce the heat to low and simmer for about 10-15 minutes, until the bread softens and starts to break down, creating a thickened soup base. In a separate small saucepan, melt the butter over medium heat. Stir in the flour and cocoa powder (if using), and cook, stirring constantly, for 1-2 minutes to make a roux.

Gradually whisk in the roux into the bread soup, stirring constantly to avoid lumps. Stir in the sugar, cinnamon stick, cardamom pods, and salt to the soup, and simmer for another 10-15 minutes, stirring occasionally, to allow the flavors to meld. Remove the cinnamon stick and cardamom pods from the soup before serving. Serve the Leivasupp hot, garnished with a dollop of whipped cream (if desired) and enjoy the comforting flavors of this traditional Estonian bread soup!

Vahukoor-Kohupiimakook

Preparation time: 20 minutes
Nutrition facts (per serving): 331 Cal (16g fat, 4g protein, 2g fiber)

Vahukoor-kohupiimakook, or Estonian Whipped Cream and Curd Cheese Cake, is a popular dessert in Estonia that combines the rich creaminess of whipped cream with the tangy freshness of curd cheese. It's a no-bake cake that's chilled in the refrigerator, making it easy to prepare and perfect for warm weather or special occasions.

Ingredients (8 servings)
Crust
8 oz. digestive biscuits or graham crackers
3 ½ oz. unsalted butter, melted

Filling
1 lb. curd cheese or quark
2 cups heavy whipping cream
4 oz. powdered sugar
1 teaspoon vanilla extract
Zest of 1 lemon
1 teaspoon gelatin powder
3 tablespoons cold water

Fresh berries, sliced fruits or chocolate shavings, for decoration

Preparation

Crush the digestive biscuits or graham crackers into fine crumbs using a food processor or by placing them in a plastic bag and crushing them with a rolling pin. In a suitable mixing bowl, mix the biscuit or cracker crumbs with the melted butter, and stir until this mixture resembles wet sand. Press the crumb mixture firmly into the bottom of a 9-inch springform pan, forming an even crust. Place the pan in the refrigerator to chill while you prepare the filling.

In a suitable bowl, drizzle the gelatin powder over the cold water, and let it sit for a few minutes to bloom. In a suitable mixing bowl, mix the curd cheese or quark, heavy whipping cream, powdered sugar, vanilla extract, and lemon zest. Whisk or beat with an electric mixer until smooth and creamy. In a suitable saucepan, gently heat the bloomed gelatin mixture over low heat, stirring constantly, until the gelatin is completely dissolved. Gradually pour the dissolved gelatin into the curd cheese mixture while whisking or beating continuously, until well combined. Pour the filling over the chilled crust in the springform pan, and smooth the top with a spatula.

Cover the pan with plastic wrap and refrigerate for at least 4-6 hours, until the cake is set and firm. Once the cake is chilled and set, carefully remove the sides of the springform pan. Decorate the top of the cake with fresh berries, sliced fruits, or chocolate shavings, if desired. Slice and serve the Vahukoor-kohupiimakook, and enjoy the creamy, tangy, and luscious flavors of this delightful Estonian dessert!

Potato Cake (Kartulikook)

Preparation time: 10 minutes
Cook time: 62 minutes
Nutrition facts (per serving): 161 Cal (0.4g fat, 0.2g protein, 1.1g fiber)

Estonian Potato Cake is traditionally served as a dessert or a sweet treat, but it can also be enjoyed as a breakfast or brunch dish. It's a unique and tasty dish that's popular in Estonia, especially during holidays and celebrations.

Ingredients (8 servings)
Crust
2 cups all-purpose flour
1 cup unsalted butter, chilled and cubed
½ cup sugar, granulated
¼ teaspoon salt
1 large egg yolk

Filling
2 lbs. potatoes, peeled and boiled until fork-tender
½ cup unsalted butter, melted
½ cup sugar, granulated
3 large eggs
1 cup sour cream
1 teaspoon vanilla extract

½ teaspoon ground cinnamon

¼ teaspoon ground nutmeg

1 pinch of salt

Preparation

Crust

At 350°F, preheat your oven and grease a 9-inch springform pan. To make the crust, mix the sugar, flour, salt, and cubed butter in a suitable mixing bowl. Use a pastry cutter or your fingers to cut the butter into the dry ingredients until this mixture resembles coarse crumbs. Stir in the egg yolk until this dough comes together. Press this dough evenly into the bottom of the prepared springform pan to form the crust. Bake the crust in the preheated oven for 10-12 minutes, until lightly golden brown. Remove from the oven and leave it to cool slightly.

Filling

Mash the boiled potatoes in a suitable mixing bowl until smooth. Stir in the melted butter, sugar, eggs, sour cream, vanilla extract, cinnamon, nutmeg, and a pinch of salt to the mashed potatoes. Stir until well combined. Pour the potato filling over the partially baked crust in the springform pan. Smooth the top with a spatula and bake in the preheated oven for 45-50 minutes, until the center is set and the top is lightly golden brown. Remove the potato cake from the oven and leave it to cool completely in the pan. Once cooled, carefully remove the sides of the springform pan. Cut the Estonian Potato Cake into slices and serve chilled or at room temperature. Enjoy your delicious Estonian Potato Cake!

Kamavaht

Preparation time: 15 minutes
Nutrition facts (per serving): 221 Cal (11g fat, 4g protein, 1.4g fiber)

Kamavaht, or Estonian Kama Cream, is a popular Estonian dessert that's made from kama, a traditional roasted grain mixture, and whipped cream. This creamy and slightly tangy dessert is easy to make and can be enjoyed as a sweet treat after a meal or as a light and refreshing dessert.

Ingredients (2 servings)
½ cup Kama mixture (roasted grain powder, available in Estonian or specialty food stores)
1 cup heavy whipping cream
¼ cup sugar, powdered
1 teaspoon vanilla extract

Preparation
In a suitable mixing bowl, mix the Kama mixture, powdered sugar, and vanilla extract. Stir well to ensure even distribution of the ingredients. In a separate bowl, whip the heavy cream until it thickens and forms soft peaks. Gently fold the whipped cream into the Kama mixture, using a spatula or a whisk. Be careful not to overmix, as you want to keep this mixture light and airy. Taste the Kamavaht and adjust the sweetness with more powdered sugar, if desired. Spoon the Kamavaht into individual serving dishes or dessert glasses. Chill the Kamavaht in the refrigerator for at least 1 hour before serving. Serve the Kamavaht chilled, and garnish with additional Kama powder or fresh berries, if desired. Enjoy the creamy and tangy flavors of Kamavaht, a delicious Estonian dessert made

with Kama and whipped cream. It's a unique and refreshing treat that's sure to delight your taste buds!

Kama and Apple Cake (Kama-Õunakook)

Preparation time: 20 minutes
Cook time: 45 minutes
Nutrition facts (per serving): 317 Cal (17g fat, 5g protein, 0.8g fiber)

Kama-õunakook, or Estonian Kama and Apple Cake, is a delicious dessert that combines the unique flavor of Kama, a traditional roasted grain mixture, with sweet apples. This cake is moist, aromatic, and perfect for enjoying with a cup of coffee or tea.

Ingredients (8 servings)
Cake
3 medium apples, peeled, cored, and thinly sliced
1 ½ cups all-purpose flour
½ cup Kama mixture (roasted grain powder, available in Estonian or specialty food stores)
½ cup sugar, granulated
½ cup unsalted butter, softened
2 large eggs
½ cup milk
1 teaspoon baking powder
1 teaspoon vanilla extract
¼ teaspoon salt

Topping

¼ cup all-purpose flour

¼ cup sugar, granulated

2 tablespoons unsalted butter, chilled and cut into small cubes

Preparation

At 350°F, preheat your oven and grease a 9-inch round cake pan. In a suitable bowl, whisk the flour, Kama, baking powder, and salt. In a separate large bowl, cream together the butter and sugar until light and fluffy. Beat in the eggs, one by one, then stir in the vanilla extract. Gradually stir in the dry flour mixture to the butter mixture, alternating with the milk, beginning and ending with the dry ingredients. Mix until just combined. Pour the prepared batter into the prepared cake pan and spread it out evenly. Arrange the thinly sliced apples on top of the prepared batter, overlapping them slightly.

In a suitable bowl, mix together the flour and sugar for the topping. Cut in the chilled butter using a pastry cutter or your fingertips until this mixture resembles coarse crumbs. Drizzle the topping evenly over the apples. Bake the cake in the preheated oven for 40-45 minutes, until a toothpick inserted into the center comes out clean.

Remove the cake from the oven and leave it to cool in the pan for 10 minutes, then place it onto the wire rack to cool completely. Once cooled, slice the Kama-õunakook into wedges and serve as a delightful Estonian dessert.

Drinks

Fruit Wine (Leibkonna Jook)

Preparation time: 20 minutes
Cook time: 15 minutes
Nutrition facts (per serving): 161 Cal (0.4g fat, 0.2g protein, 1.1g fiber)

Estonian Leibkonna jook, also known as homemade fruit or berry wine, is a traditional fermented beverage that is often enjoyed during festive occasions or special events. It's made by fermenting fruits or berries with sugar and water to create a sweet and slightly alcoholic drink.

Ingredients (8 servings)
2 lbs. fresh fruits or berries (apples, cherries, currants, raspberries)
2 lbs. sugar
16 cups water
1 teaspoon fresh yeast or ½ teaspoon dry yeast

Preparation
Wash and clean the fruits or berries, removing any stems, leaves, or pits. Crush or mash them slightly to release the juices. In a suitable pot, mix the fruits or berries, sugar, and water. Stir well to dissolve the sugar. Bring this mixture to a boil over medium heat, then reduce the heat and simmer for about 10-15 minutes, stirring occasionally.

Remove the pot from the heat and let this mixture cool to room temperature. Once this mixture has cooled, dissolve the yeast in a suitable amount of water and add it to the pot. Stir well. Cover the pot with a clean cloth or plastic wrap and let it sit at room temperature for 24 hours to ferment. After 24 hours, strain this mixture through a fine mesh strainer or cheesecloth into clean bottles, leaving some headspace at the top. Seal the bottles tightly with caps or corks and store them in a cool, dark place for at least 2-3 weeks to allow the Leibkonna jook to ferment and develop its flavors.

After 2-3 weeks, the Leibkonna jook should be ready to drink. Chill it in the refrigerator before serving, and enjoy it as a refreshing and traditional Estonian homemade beverage during special occasions or celebrations.

Kvas

Preparation time: 15 minutes
Nutrition facts (per serving): 130 Cal (3g fat, 2 protein, 0.3g fiber)

Kvas is a traditional fermented beverage popular in many Eastern European countries, including Estonia. It's made from fermented rye bread and is known for its refreshing, tangy taste.

Ingredients (8 servings)
9 oz. rye bread (preferably stale or slightly dried)
16 cups water
4 oz. sugar
1 teaspoon fresh yeast or ½ teaspoon dry yeast
1-2 small lemons, thinly sliced
2 handfuls of raisins or dried fruits for added flavor (optional)

Preparation
Cut the rye bread into small cubes and place them in a suitable pot or bowl. Add 16 cups of water to the pot with the rye bread and let it sit at room temperature for 4-6 hours, or overnight, to steep. After steeping, strain the liquid from the rye bread, pressing down on the bread cubes to extract as much liquid as possible. Discard the bread or save it for other uses.

Dissolve the sugar in the strained liquid, stirring well to ensure it's fully dissolved. In a suitable bowl, dissolve the yeast in a suitable amount of water and add it to the liquid. Stir well. Stir in the thinly sliced lemon slices and optional raisins or dried fruits to the liquid. Cover the pot or bowl with a clean cloth or plastic wrap and let it sit at room temperature for 6-12 hours to ferment.

Once the fermentation is complete, strain the liquid through a fine mesh strainer or cheesecloth into clean bottles, leaving some headspace at the top. Seal the bottles tightly with caps or corks and refrigerate them for at least 2-3 days to allow the Kvas to carbonate and develop its flavors. After 2-3 days, the Kvas should be ready to drink. Chill it in the refrigerator before serving, and enjoy it as a refreshing and tangy traditional Estonian beverage.

Kefir

Preparation time: 15 minutes
Nutrition facts (per serving): 145 Cal (4.4g fat, 0.3g protein, 0g fiber)

Kefir is a popular fermented milk drink that's similar to yogurt but has a thinner consistency and a tangy flavor. It's believed to have originated in the Caucasus region and is known for its probiotic properties, which can be beneficial for gut health.

Ingredients (4 servings)
4 teaspoons Kefir grains (available online or at health food stores)
4 cups milk
Sweeteners or flavorings (honey, fruit or vanilla extract), optional

Preparation
Place the kefir grains in a clean glass jar. Add milk to the jar, leaving some headspace at the top for fermentation. Stir the milk and kefir grains gently with a non-metal spoon. Cover the jar with a clean cloth or a plastic lid, but do not seal it tightly as the fermentation process produces gas. Let the kefir ferment at room temperature for 24-48 hours, depending on your desired level of tartness. The longer you let it ferment, the tangier it will become. After fermentation, strain the kefir into another clean jar, separating the kefir grains from the liquid. You can use a fine mesh strainer or a plastic sieve for this. The strained kefir is now ready to drink, or you can add sweeteners or flavorings to taste. If you want to reuse the kefir grains to make another batch, simply add fresh milk to the jar with the kefir grains and repeat the fermentation process.

Estonian Morss

Preparation time: 10 minutes
Nutrition facts (per serving): 172 Cal (6g fat, 0.3g protein, 0g fiber)

Morss is a traditional Estonian drink made from fermented rye bread, water, and sweeteners. It's a refreshing and slightly tangy beverage that's popular in Estonia, especially during the summer months.

Ingredients (8 servings)
10 ½ oz. of rye bread
8 cups of water
½ cup of sugar
Fresh mint leaves or lemon slices, for garnish

Preparation
Cut the rye bread into small pieces and place them in a suitable bowl or pitcher. Pour the water over the rye bread, making sure that all the bread pieces are submerged. Cover this bowl or pitcher with a clean cloth or plastic wrap, and let it sit at room temperature for 12-24 hours to allow fermentation to occur. The longer you let it ferment, the tangier the Morss will be. After fermentation, strain the liquid from the rye bread using a fine mesh strainer or cheesecloth, discarding the bread solids. Stir in sugar to taste, starting with ½ cup and adjusting as needed. Chill the Morss in the refrigerator for at least 1-2 hours before serving. When serving, you can garnish the Morss with fresh mint leaves or lemon slices if desired. Stir well before serving, as the sediment may settle at the bottom.

Estonian Kali Drink

Preparation time: 10 minutes
Nutrition facts (per serving): 182 Cal (0.4g fat, 0.7g protein, 1.4g fiber)

Kali is a traditional Estonian soft drink made from fermented bread, similar to Morss. It has a sweet and slightly tangy taste and is a popular non-alcoholic beverage in Estonia.

Ingredients (8 servings)
10 ½ oz. of dark rye bread (preferably stale)
8 cups of water
½ cup of sugar
½ teaspoon of active dry yeast
Fresh mint leaves or lemon slices, for garnish

Preparation
Cut the rye bread into small pieces and place them in a suitable bowl or pitcher. Pour the water over the rye bread, making sure that all the bread pieces are submerged. Cover this bowl or pitcher with a clean cloth or plastic wrap, and let it sit at room temperature for 2-3 hours to allow fermentation to occur. After fermentation, strain the liquid from the bread using a fine mesh strainer or cheesecloth, discarding the bread solids. Stir in sugar to taste, starting with ½ cup and adjusting as needed. Dissolve the yeast in a suitable amount of warm water and add it to the strained liquid, stirring well. Cover this bowl or pitcher again and let it sit at room temperature for an additional 1-2 hours to allow the yeast to ferment and carbonate the drink. Chill the Kali in the refrigerator for at

least 1-2 hours before serving. When serving, you can garnish the Kali with fresh mint leaves or lemon slices, if desired. Stir well before serving, as the sediment may settle at the bottom.

If you liked Estonian recipes, discover to how cook DELICIOUS recipes from **Balkan** countries!

Within these pages, you'll learn 35 authentic recipes from a Balkan cook. These aren't ordinary recipes you'd find on the Internet, but recipes that were closely guarded by our Balkan mothers and passed down from generation to generation.

Main Dishes, Appetizers, and Desserts included!

If you want to learn how to make Croatian green peas stew, and 32 other authentic Balkan recipes, then start with our book!

Order at www.balkanfood.org/cook-books/ for only $2,99

Maybe Hungarian cuisine?

Order at www.balkanfood.org/cook-books/ for only $2,99

If you're a **Mediterranean** dieter who wants to know the secrets of the Mediterranean diet, dieting, and cooking, then you're about to discover how to master cooking meals on a Mediterranean diet right now!

In fact, if you want to know how to make Mediterranean food, then this new e-book - "The 30-minute Mediterranean diet" - gives you the answers to many important questions and challenges every Mediterranean dieter faces, including:

- How can I succeed with a Mediterranean diet?
- What kind of recipes can I make?
- What are the key principles to this type of diet?
- What are the suggested weekly menus for this diet?
- Are there any cheat items I can make?

... and more!

If you're serious about cooking meals on a Mediterranean diet and you really want to know how to make Mediterranean food, then you need to grab a copy of "The 30-minute Mediterranean diet" right now.

Prepare **111 recipes with several ingredients in less than 30 minutes**!

Order at www.balkanfood.org/cook-books/ for only $2,99

What could be better than a home-cooked meal? Maybe only a **Greek** homemade meal.

Do not get discouraged if you have no Greek roots or friends. Now you can make a Greek food feast in your kitchen.

This ultimate Greek cookbook offers you 111 best dishes of this cuisine! From more famous gyros to more exotic *Kota Kapama* this cookbook keeps it easy and affordable.

All the ingredients necessary are wholesome and widely accessible. The author's picks are as flavorful as they are healthy. The dishes described in this cookbook are "what Greek mothers have made for decades."

Full of well-balanced and nutritious meals, this handy cookbook includes many vegan options. Discover a plethora of benefits of Mediterranean cuisine, and you may fall in love with cooking at home.

Inspired by a real food lover, this collection of delicious recipes will taste buds utterly satisfied.

Order at www.balkanfood.org/cook-books/ for only $2,99

Maybe some Swedish meatballs ?

Order at www.balkanfood.org/cook-books/ for only $2,99

Maybe to try exotic **Syrian** cuisine?

From succulent *sarma*, soups, warm and cold salads to delectable desserts, the plethora of flavors will satisfy the most jaded foodie. Have a taste of a new culture with this **traditional Syrian cookbook**.

Order at www.balkanfood.org/cook-books/ for only $2,99

Maybe **Polish** cuisine?

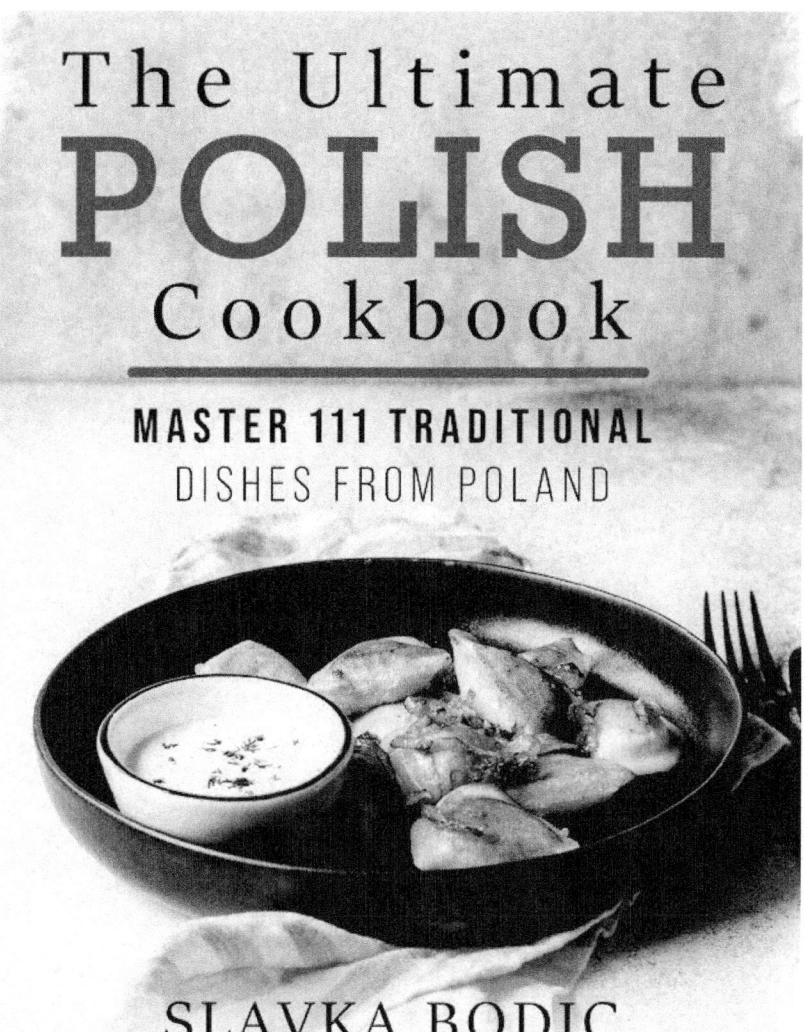

Order at www.balkanfood.org/cook-books/ for only $2,99

Or **Peruvian**?

Order at www.balkanfood.org/cook-books/ for only $2,99

ONE LAST THING

If you enjoyed this book or found it useful, I'd be very grateful if you could find the time to post a short review on Amazon. Your support really does make a difference and I read all the reviews personally, so I can get your feedback and make this book even better.

Thanks again for your support!

Please send me your feedback at

www.balkanfood.org

Printed in Dunstable, United Kingdom